A Century of Caring

1893 - 1993

*Best Wishes
Bob R*

A History of the Guelph Humane Society

By Bob Rutter

A Century of Caring

© **1993 by The Guelph Humane Society, Inc.**
ALL RIGHTS RESERVED

ISBN: 1-879260-13-1

> The Guelph Humane Society, Inc.
> P.O. Box 684
> 500 Wellington St.
> Guelph, Ontario N1H 6L3

Cover Photo Credits
Front: Guelph Humane Society
Back: Ross Davidson-Pilon

Table of Contents

Introduction 1

Attitudes toward humanity 5

The Early Years 11
    Prevention of cruelty, protection of children and animals was goal 11
    Society president wrote original law to protect children 12
    Cruelty to animals came in many forms 14
    Demon Drink was chief culprit of family abuse 16
    Founding Officers of the Guelph Humane Society 17
    Kindness to all 18

A strong leadership 26
    Frank Cooke 26
    Maude Pentelow 28
    Sandra Jefferies Bond 32

Search for an animal shelter begins 35
    Humane Society is Busy Organization 36

Pressure for change 40

A question of jurisdicton 55

Demand escalates need for new facility 65

Animal advocacy 78

A final word 83

Officers of the Guelph Humane Society 87

Abbreviations used in the text

AHA	American Humane Association
AHT	Animal health technician
CCAC	Canadian Council on Animal Care
CFHS	Canadian Federation of Humane Societies
GHS	Guelph Humane Society
OSPCA	Ontario Society for the Prevention of Cruelty to Animals
OAC	Ontario Agricultural College
OVC	Ontario Veterinary College
RSPA	Royal Society for the Prevention of Cruelty to Animals
SPCA	Society for the Prevention of Cruelty to Animals
THS	Toronto Humane Society
VHT	Veterinary health technician

*"It shall not be lawful to destroy in any way any native toad (**bufo lentignosus**) or to wantonly or unnecessarily injure or destroy the spawn, or larvae thereof in streams or ponds of water."*
Unsuccessful bill placed before the Ontario legislature in 1888 by John Leys, MPP[1]

Introduction

The quest for truth, especially that which is enveloped in the mists of time, is much like a jigsaw puzzle. A few pieces can form a whole, or lead to many new inquiries for additional playing pieces, and that is how this project progressed. From a few fragments of information has grown the story that follows. I hope that it will become both a historical document, and an inspiration to those in the Guelph Humane Society (GHS) who will follow the steps first trod by the dedicated members who worked to make the Society a vital part of our community.

Why is there a need for a humane society? A passage written by Freda Davies in an article in the 1961 Canadian Federation of Humane Societies Journal probably comes the closest to adequately answering the question:

"By every instance of degrading cruelty which we condone, we hasten the danger of destruction of body, mind and soul but by every act of uplifting mercy which we encourage, we strengthen the powers which alone can achieve that peaceful way of life which man has sought down the long years."

Even though I have been involved with the humane movement for the past 20 years, I found myself challenging my own commitment in the face of the overwhelming dedication, compassion and work by those who founded and set the Guelph Humane Society on its present course a century ago. It has been humbling experience.

If there is a failing in the work that follows, it is mine. I have tried to locate as many sources as possible to provide as clear a picture of the Society's first century of service. But, as in all attempts at reconstructing the past, there are gaps caused by a lack of source material. There are two ways to view the society's history: periods when a shelter was being planned, opened or expanded; or, as the story of one of the three significant individuals who guided the Society's development over the years.

During the period 1965 to 1974 there is little documented material aside from the Frank Cooke papers. I was unable to locate minutes of meetings for a period after 1967, and had to rely on correspondence and documents contained in the Cooke papers, conversations with people and what little could be gleaned from media sources. The task of seeking infor-

---
[1] *Aims and Objects of the Toronto Humane Society.* p. 77

A Century of Caring

mation on the early days was also hampered by a lack of newspaper records which were destroyed by fire during the early part of the century.

There are many who must be acknowledged for opening doors, or for filling in the gaps that remained after the preliminary work was done. Without these people, who gave generously of time, advice and assistance, I would not have completed this task. They are numerous, and I am indebted to them all.

I must offer a heartfelt thank you to the family of the late Frank Cooke, especially the late Mrs. Nancy Cooke, who graciously allowed me access to the minute books, papers and other records that had remained with the family. And, I acknowledge the assistance of my former Daily Mercury colleague Eric Colwill, who stood in for me during an interview with Mrs. Cooke.

Jean Forsythe and Al Koop, at the Family and Children's Services, assisted me with research into the early days of the Society, opening up files and documents – including allowing me access to the original draft minutes of the charter meeting on Nov. 17, 1893 and the original handwritten draft constitution. Without their assistance, I might not have been able to capture the detail and the flavor of the GHS's first third of a century.

Those who kept me looking in the right corners and deserve special thanks include Linda Kearns and Susan Waterman of the Guelph Public Library, Ellen Morrison and Nancy Sadak of the University of Guelph archives, Robin Etherington, director of the Guelph Civic Museum, and Harry Worton, retired member of the legislature for Guelph, baker and former mayor, who offered an insight into the early days of the Junior Humane Society of GHS.

Rick Koury, operations manager and senior inspector, and Brian Denham, executive director, of the Ontario Society for the Prevention of Cruelty to Animals, and Frances Rodenburg, executive director of the Canadian Federation of Humane Societies, were most helpful in assisting me by providing me access to whatever material they had available.

A special acknowledgment, however, must be made to Charles D. Nivens, whose book *A History of the Humane Movement* I discovered in the National Library. The book proved a valuable source of information. I recommend it, especially for those interested in the theological arguments Nivens advances about the role of religion in the humane movement.

Suffice it to say, I am also indebted to the GHS membership, past and present, who gave so much to assist me in my endeavors.

However, it is the Guelph Humane Society that deserves the greatest thanks. They have provided assistance, support, and publication of this work. Equally important, however, is that without its existence, I would not have had the opportunity to embark on this journey of discovery. It has been an enjoyable exercise, and one that I will treasure.

This book is dedicated to the Guelph Humane Society, and to all those who will lead it in the future. May they never lose sight of the ideals upon which it was founded in 1893.

    Bob Rutter,
    Guelph, Ontario
    September, 1992

> "No civilization is complete which does not include within its sphere of charity and mercy the dumb and defenseless of God's creatures."
> *Queen Victoria, 1887*

Attitudes toward humanity

Guelph Humane Society's early humanitarian efforts were meant to build on a public sentiment that favored social assistance of the defenseless. There was a perception prevalent that a significant new social order had been, or was on the verge of being achieved. This is illustrated by a comment made at the 1887 annual meeting of the American Humane Association: "Law and public sentiment and active supervision have made cruelty, which was once commonplace treatment of the animal, a disgrace and a crime."[1]

The organized humane movement had been active in the United Kingdom and the British Empire since the mid-18th Century, a fact that gives rise to many people believing it was the birthplace of the movement. But there is evidence that parts of Europe and Scandinavia were making considerable progress while debate raged in England over laws to protect animals. Even earlier, it seems that a code of conduct respecting the rights of animals dates back to the Old Testament of The Bible. So Britain's claim to the birthplace of the humane movement is open to question.

Where, when, or with whom the honor rests is a subjective and controversial question. To illustrate the difficulty in isolating the moment in history where the values of humanity toward the birds and beasts took place, one only has to turn to the book *History of the Humane Movement* written by Charles D. Nivens, a humane advocate who helped establish the Eastern Ontario SPCA. Nivens opens his book with the suggestion that Moses is the first identified person in history who promoted humanitarian values; and that he might be the real father of our present-day humane movement.[2] If we accept Nivens' suggestion, then the humane movement could date from the early Egyptians. Even so, the extent to which the early civilizations accepted humanity toward animals appears limited only to those animals that provided a benefit to man. Nivens notes, for instance, that the Jewish code of laws at the time of Moses "was just emerging from the idea of child sacrifice and had certainly not given up the idea of animal sacrifice, (but) one finds two or three laws which provide for the humane treatment of animals which helped man in laborious agricultural tasks."[3]

Christian attitudes of compassion toward animals were formed chiefly by the churches, although the Roman Catholic church, despite the well-known roles played by St. Francis of Assisi and Pope Pius V, failed to

---

[1] Last report of the general society of the American Humane Association, held at Rochester, N.Y., October, 1887.
[2] *A History of the Humane Movement*, by Chas. D. Nivens, published by Transatlantic Arts Inc. New York, 1967, p 9.
[3] ibid. p 10.

make significant gains in Spain where the practice of bull-fighting continues to this day.

Meanwhile, in England, there is no way but to describe the life of animals until the 17th century as little more than a living hell. Bull- and dog-baiting, cock- and dog-fighting and over-working of horses were commonplace. By the mid-17th century after the birth of George Fox in 1624, the founder of the Quaker Movement, efforts to protect animals became stronger. People began to question and criticize practices of animal abuse that had been taken for granted. In less than two centuries, England went from this living hell to the world's leading country in the field of humane legislation. This was due in part to the role of clergy, particularly John Wesley, the great theologian who believed animals had souls, and preached that "something better remains after death for these poor creatures..." He was joined by many in raising awareness of the callous acts against animals in the name of sport or recreation.

However, the turning point for the English movement came in 1776 when Dr. Humphrey Primatt published *A Dissertation on the Duty of Mercy and Sin of Cruelty to Brute Animals*, the first book devoted entirely to the teaching of kindness toward animals. Primatt's book is viewed by the Royal Society for the Prevention of Cruelty to Animals as a cornerstone of the organization because of its influence on those who were to establish the society almost 50 years later.[4] The Church of England, which actively embraced the expression of humane values during the debate leading up to and following the passage of anti-cruelty legislation in 1822, was joined by the Quakers in the fight to end cruelty and the baiting of animals for sport. It must be remembered that England in the 18th century was still very much a country of brutality; not just toward animals, but also toward children who labored 70 or 80 hours a week without legal rights or sympathy.[5]

Pope Pius V came to the defence of bulls in 1567 by refusing a 'cape d'honneur' and a million pesetas gift from the bull-fighters of Seville. Pius also decreed that "bulls or wild beasts baited in the circus or forum (was a practice) contrary to Christian duty and charity...," Participants at a circus or forum were threatened with excommunication. But Pius went farther: "We forbid soldiers and all other persons, whether on foot or on horseback, to dare to contend with bulls or other beasts in the aforementioned exhibitions. And if any one of them meets his death there he shall be deprived of Christian burial..."[6] But the bull-fighters of Spain were not listening. While Pius helped to further the cause of humane attitudes, he failed to achieve any degree of success in Spain where "bull-fighters in Seville...have their Madonna and their church (and) they see no *sin* in bull-fighting."[7]

Meanwhile, the momentum of the humane movement in France appeared to have been lost over the great philosophers preoccupation with

---

[4] ibid. p 53.
[5] Typescript A Brief Summary of the Humane Movement by K.G. Switzer, managing director of the Ottawa Humane Society, no date. Located in the files of the Canadian Federation of Humane Societies, Ottawa. Switzer makes an interesting comment about English attitudes at the time when he discusses the efforts of Richard Martin, who he calls the father of the modern humane movement: "Martin also introduced a bill that would have allowed legal counsel to persons accused of capital crimes. The bill was defeated chiefly by the argument that if accused people had lawyers, the courts would never be able to get through their business."
[6] Nivens, ibid. p 44. Extracts from the *Bull De Salute Gregis*, 1 Nov. 1567 (Trans.) The Latin original is in the London (England) Library vol. 2. p 260 of *Magnum Bullarium Romanum*. Reprinted in the Church and Kindness to Animals (Burns and Oates, 1916).
[7] ibid. p 32. No emphasis added.

defining life, both the physical and spiritual. St. Thomas Aquinas, the great Catholic thinker, and Rene Descartes, the noted French mathematician and philosopher, both accepted the concept that animals were automatons, and thus without feeling. Descartes, especially, linked his great philosophical assumption: "I think, therefore I am," to animal welfare and "persuaded himself that anything or any creature which could not think did not feel!"

But most damaging was the philosophy of St. Thomas. In his essay *Summa Contra Gentiles*, he accepts the right of man to take out his frustrations on an animal if it prevents this anger from injuring another person, or causing some loss to the victim.[8] St. Thomas's teachings were formally adopted by Pope Leo XIII in 1880. And, although not binding on the faith, the acceptance of Thomasism created an official doctrine, which Nivens says "permits an individual (Catholic) to be considered a good Christian even though he is actively cruel to animals."[9][10]

Richard Martin, an Irish aristocrat and English MP born in 1754, is generally credited with being the father of the organized humane movement as we know it today. He introduced a bill given Royal assent in 1822, to protect horses, sheep and cattle. Twenty-two years earlier in 1800, Sir W. Pulteney had tried unsuccessfully to pass a bill through Westminster to prevent the baiting of bulls, a favorite pastime of the masses. In 1809, Lord Erskine managed to have a bill to prevent cruelty to animals passed by the House of Lords – but it was rejected by the House of Commons. A year later, Erskine again tried unsuccessfully with a similar bill.[11]

Long before these events in England, animal welfare and humane values were being adopted in Germany and in Sweden. While Martin deserves the recognition he's received, there are some who believe the real pioneering work of the modern humane movement took place in Germany and Sweden.[12] Nivens argues that England required the passing of the anti-cruelty law of 1822 to protect animals because the United Kingdom was a constitutional monarchy which demanded formal approvals; whereas the monarchs in Germany and Sweden had autocratic powers that resulted in decrees which informally protected animals from mistreatment. In other words, democracy for the masses enjoyed in the United Kingdom actually delayed and slowed the movement toward a more caring, humane society!

As early as 1417, the city-state of Cologne, Germany, had a law protecting nightingales, which were a favorite target of hunters along their annual migration routes from northern Italy.[13] In 1766, a team driver was

---

[8] ibid. p 31. Nivens quotes St. Thomas: "If in the Holy Scriptures there are found some injunctions forbidding the infliction of cruelty towards brute animals. . . this is either for removing a man's mind from exercising cruelty to other men, lest anyone, from exercising upon brutes should go on hence to human beings; or because the injury inflicted on animals turns to a temporal loss for some man, either the person who inflicts the injury or some other; or some other meaning as the apostle expounds (in) Deut. 25, 4."

[9] ibid. pp. 31-32.

[10] As late as the 1970s, according to an undated newspaper clipping located in the Frank Cooke papers, the Catholic Register was speaking out against opponents of the proposed Ontario Animals for Research Act and in support of the use of stray pets for research projects, although more because of what it viewed as scare tactics than for philosophical reasons. The United Church Observer also condemned the opponents of the Bill for having failed to read the legislation. People were "deceived by expensive advertising into thinking their pets were to be subjected to 'staggering torture by icy-hearted scientists.' They wrote angry letters, signed petitions in churches and got mad at ministers who didn't preach on it."

[11] Switzer writes that Martin was not a meek man having participated in six duels, "killing one man and puncturing five." As magistrate of his family's 200,000 acre estate, and later as High Sheriff of County Galway, Ireland, Martin "outlawed bull-baiting, cock-fighting, dog-fighting and similar abuses of animals. He had no real law behind him but applied the principle that the law is what the courts say it is." When Martin turned over his estates in 1824 to his son, it was discovered that he had been quietly supporting a large number of aged peasants and 30 orphans through pensions. No one knows why or how he came to be generous and benevolent. King George IV called him: "Humanity Martin", an especially fitting accolade.

[12] Nivens, ibid. p 97.

sentenced to twelve weeks in prison by a Leipzig court for riding a horse to death. "By contrast, in the year 1848 – that is to say 82 years after this Leipzig case and, incidentally, 26 years after England had a formal anti-cruelty law – a rider was fined *only a small amount* for riding a mare nearly 100 miles in 11 and 3/4 hours." The ride was undertaken as a bet and the mare died soon after the race ended. Baiting of animals was not stopped in England until 1835 while Kaiser Joseph II stopped the practice in Germany in 1789.[14]

In 1824, the Royal Society for the Prevention of Cruelty to Animals (RSPCA) was founded by Rev. Arthur Broome, a Church of England minister.[15] Broome, secretary of the RSPCA, had single-handedly carried on his work of preventing cruelty to animals for several years before the formation of the society. When the RSCPA was formed, Broome give up his calling to the church to work full-time for the newly-created society. Living off his own financial resources, it took barely two years for Broome and the society to become mired in serious financial difficulties. As secretary and treasurer of the new SPCA, he was held responsible for its debts and, accordingly, he was sent to debtor's prison in 1826. He was saved the humiliation of a long term in jail, however, after the debts were paid by Richard Martin and Lewis Gompertz, a Jewish writer, who were both founding members of the society.[16]

Queen Victoria, who became a major force in bringing about reforms for both animals and children, was named patron of the Society for the Prevention of Cruelty to Animals in 1835. She was, as Nivens states, "personally involved" in its operations. When Victoria was crowned in 1837, she bestowed the prefix Royal on the society, a move that helped promote its goals throughout the British Empire and provided a momentum the movement desperately needed to achieve wide acceptance. The regal endorsement was of profound importance for the RSCPA because it came at the moment when it was struggling to raise money to stay alive after losing the largesse of Lewis Gompertz. Victoria's personal role in supporting the humane cause included speaking out against the killing of birds to supply colorful feathers to adorn women's hats; and the need to recognize the emotional role animals played in a compassionate society.

The extent to which Victoria held a commitment to animal welfare is illustrated by comments to Lord Carnarvon, author of the anti-vivisectionist Cruelty to Animals Act of 1876 in Great Britain. The queen referred to "the horrible, disgraceful and unChristian vivisection" of animals in a letter to console him on the death of his mother shortly after he introduced the bill at Westminster.[17]

Real growth in public sentiment and support wasn't forthcoming, however, until the period 1860 to 1885 when the number of humane organizations around the world grew to more than 400 from fewer than 10.[18] This

---

[13] ibid. p 98 "Although the formal passing of a law for the protection of cruelty to animals was slightly later in Germany than in England, cruelty could be suppressed more easily in Germany than in England without formal law because of the absolute power each of the kingdoms of Germany. If the monarch happened to be a humane man, cruelty was put down in short order."
[14] Switzer, ibid.
[15] Helping Hands, The First Century; A history of the Ottawa Humane Society; p 9.
[16] Nivens, ibid. Martin was Roman Catholic, a fact that suggests the creation of the SPCA could be the first truly ecumenical undertaking in the name of humanity. But any such suggestion would be wrong. A little more than a decade later Gompertz, who had taken over the operation of the SPCA and personally financed its operation for six years, resigned after the society passed a resolution, clearly directed at him, that "the proceedings of the society were entirely based on Christian faith and Christian principles."
[17] Undated RSPCA report on the Vivisection Act written by The Hon. Juliet Gardner, granddaughter of Lord Carnarvon.

was partly the result of Victoria's continued support but more a direct result of the efforts of Henry Bergh, a U.S. diplomat and philanthropist inspired by the success of the RSPCA.

Bergh began the first American SPCA in New York in 1866, a remarkable achievement considering it was done within the space of four years – 1862-66, and during a period in which he also served with the U.S. legation in St. Petersburg, Russia.[19] This precedent-making event in North America was followed two years later by the creation of the first Canadian society, The Canadian Society for the Prevention of Cruelty to Animals, based in Montreal. (The society continues today under the same name, although its activities are confined to the Montreal area.) And one year after the Canadian SPCA came into being, Parliament passed the Dominion Cruelty to Animals Act of 1869. It was followed in 1875 by a second law making it a crime to abuse or neglect animals in transit.[20]

In 1866, New York State became what has been generally believed to be the first North American jurisdiction to have a comprehensive anti-cruelty and animal protection law, the direct result of Bergh's efforts.[21] But this is not completely accurate. Nova Scotia passed two anti-cruelty laws in 1822, and again in 1824, which provided for public whipping as a punishment.[22] There is also a report that an anti-cruelty law existed in New England as early as 1641.[23]

But it was the New York state law that was soon adopted by communities and governments throughout the continent. The New York law read:

> "Every person who shall by his act or neglect, maliciously kill, maim, wound, injure, torture or cruelly beat any horse, mule, cow, cattle, sheep or other animal belonging to himself or another, shall upon conviction be adjudged guilty of a misdemeanor."[24]

While the New York law made cruelty a misdemeanor, the Canadian laws of 1869 and 1875 were more comprehensive and made cruelty a criminal act. The Cruelty to Animals Act as it was written in 1892:

> "Whoever wantonly, cruelly, or unnecessarily beats, ill-treats, abuses, over-drives, or tortures any horse, cow, sheep, or other cattle, or any poultry, or any dog or domestic animal or bird, shall upon being convicted before the police magistrate, be punished by imprisonment for a term not exceeding three months or by a fine not exceeding $50, or by both."[25]

In 1877, the American Humane Association was formed. It was to become a dominant force in the expansion of humane societies throughout the United States and Canada.[26] The AHA would also play an important role in recognizing the Guelph Humane Society when it named Society president Frank Cooke in 1952 the first Canadian to be awarded the Still

---

[18] M.V. B. Davis, secretary of the Pennsylvania SPCA, in a letter to the 1887 AHA annual meeting. Source: THS Aims and Objects, 1888.
[19] Nivens, ibid. p 108.
[20] Compendium of Dominion Laws of Canada 1867-1883 In Force on the First Day of January, 1884; By Jules Joseph Taschereau Fremont; Located in the National Library, Ottawa; microfiche CC4-03254; ISBN 0-665-03254-4.
[21] p 10; Helping Hands, The First Century, a centennial publication of the Humane Society of Ottawa-Carleton.
[22] Ibid. p 108. Source: Animal News, I2, No. 6, p 7 (Canadian SPCA, Montreal).
[23] p 12, Aims and Objects of the Toronto Humane Society, 1888. The earliest North American statute on cruelty was passed in British Colonial America in 1641, according to an 1888 report of the Massachusetts SPCA.
[24] Nivens. ibid. p 108.
[25] p 21, Toronto Humane Society annual report, 1892.
[26] The AHA held its 1888 convention in Toronto, which may account for the large amount of space devoted to its meeting in the Toronto Humane Society book, Aims and Objects.

man Medal for distinguished contribution to the work of the animal welfare movement.

By the end of the 1880s, there were 91 members of the AHA in North America, about one-quarter the number of humane societies established in the world.[27] It is interesting to note that during this period the Ontario Society for the Prevention of Cruelty to Animals was formed (in 1873) only to become defunct by the time Guelph and many other Ontario communities became actively involved child and animal welfare. OSPCA was to be resurrected. It became chartered in 1919 as the sole agency responsible in Ontario for the enforcement of cruelty of animal legislation.[28]

It's easy to see, therefore, that when the Guelph Humane Society was organized on Nov. 17, 1893, it was a product of its time. Those who gathered at the city council chambers that evening to create the society were dedicated to protecting innocent children, helping dumb animals and determined to make Guelph a more compassionate and caring community. More important, the gathering of prominent citizens who began this local crusade against cruelty joined a world-wide humane movement which was backed up by "a vast army of God-serving, high-minded men and women."[29]

---

[27] By the mid-1880s humane societies were established in North America, Europe and India. The Calcutta SPCA reported 7,126 prosecutions and 7,042 convictions during 1886 which was "by far the largest number obtained by a society in the world," reported the Toronto Humane Society in its 1888 publication, Aims and Objects.
[28] ibid.
[29] M.V.B. Davis, secretary Pennsylvania SPCA, in a letter to the 1887 annual meeting of the American Humane Association. Source: Pg. 41, Aims and Objects of the Toronto Humane Society, 1888.

"The worst sins towards our fellow creatures is not to hate them, but to be indifferent to them. That's the essence of inhumanity."
George Bernard Shaw

The Early Years

Today the Guelph Humane Society speaks solely for animal welfare and the prevention of cruelty to animals. Yet, 100 years ago, it included in its mandate the protection of small children, a role it retained for 33 years. Guelph's dual role as advocate for children and a voice for animals was not unusual.

Surprisingly, during the past 100 years, the name of the Guelph Humane Society often became a concern, changing several times by resolution. In most cases the name changes reflected the dual role of animal welfare and children's services while others acknowledged the society's authority to operate outside Guelph within the boundaries of Wellington County.

In the draft minutes of the original meeting Nov. 17, 1893, written in the pencil of William Tytler, the society is called ***The Guelph Humane Society***. But in an order-in-council dated Jan. 29, 1894, the name is listed as the ***Humane Society of Guelph***.[1]

What sparked the meeting held Nov. 17, 1893, which resulted in the formation of the Guelph Humane Society appears lost in history. There is a reference in papers held by the late Frank Cooke[2] that Lt.-Col. Nathaniel Higinbotham, a prominent Guelph businessman and civic leader who was to become the charter president, had been actively lobbying politicians in Queen's Park about the need for child welfare laws. Higinbotham had written the founding convention of the Canadian Humane Society held in Toronto in June, 1892, that a society was being formed in Guelph.[3] However, that information appears to be incorrect since it was nearly 18 months later that the society was actually formed. The reforms Higinbotham had apparently been seek-

> **Prevention of cruelty, protection of children and animals was goal**
>
> Its objects shall be to promote and develop a humane public sentiment both towards neglected, abandoned and orphaned children, and towards animals by purely educative influences in schools and through other public and private channels, and by securing the enactment and enforcement of suitable laws for the prevention of cruelty towards such children and animals; to provide such children as may be lawfully committed or entrusted to the society with suitable homes in private families and to look after their well-being; to care for, protect, take the part of; and benefit poor children and juvenile offenders and generally to advocate the claims of these to public sympathy and support.
>
> *Article II, Constitution of the Guelph Humane Society, adopted Feb. 6, 1894*

William Tytler, drafted minutes of founding meeting
Photo: Guelph Public Library

---

[1] There is little on record to indicate how the name change came about. It is possible someone who filed the incorporation papers for the society believed a more formal name would carry greater prestige and authority.
[2] Note about founding of society discovered in the first minute book of the reborn Guelph Humane Society, 1927. Author unknown.
[3] Annual report Toronto Humane Society, 1892, p 73.

A Century of Caring

Society's president wrote original law to protect children

Absalom Shade Allan, who served as president of the Guelph Humane Society for 17 years, was one of the architects of the Children's Protection Act of 1892 which helped create the child welfare law that gave birth to the society.

As a Liberal member of the legislature for Wellington County, Allan worked under the direction of J.M. Gibson, the provincial secretary, to help write the Children's Protection Act of 1892 which gave government recognition of the work of local children's aid and humane societies.

Born in 1843 at Preston, he was named for an uncle, Absalom Shade, the founder of the nearby city of Galt (now a part of the City of Cambridge). Trained as an accountant, Allan settled in Clifford where he married Kate Bullock, daughter of Captain Bullock.

Allan had a career of distinguished service to Wellington County. He became the first reeve of the Village of Clifford in 1874, a post he held for nine years. He also served as magistrate, notary public and commissioner of oaths. He was warden of Wellington County in 1884-85, two years before he entered provincial politics. He was elected to the legislature in 1886, re-elected in 1890 and defeated in 1894. He was elected sheriff in 1901.

Col. J. M. Gibson
Photo: Ontario Archives (AO 1125)

A. S. Allan
Photo: Ontario Archives (AO 1124)

ing were achieved in 1892 when the Ontario legislature passed the Children's Protection Act which formally sanctioned the role of children's aid societies.

Guelph Humane Society's decision to become an advocate for both children and animals was the result of a realistic appraisal of the ability of its organizers to successfully carry out their mandate. These concerns centred primarily around the ability of the community to raise enough funds to pay for the services the society would provide.

"For some time previously, the need of such a society had been agitated by leading citizens of Guelph," John Joseph Kelso, the first Ontario superintendent for neglected and dependent children, wrote about the organizing meeting of the Guelph society, which he attended.[4] "And as it was extremely doubtful that the city could maintain both a humane society and a children's aid society, it was advisable to amalgamate the two movements."[5] The ultimate separation of children and animal welfare responsibilities in 1926 was inevitable, although the scope of the escalating demands for children's aid services was well beyond the imagination of those who created the organization in 1893.

Although the Guelph society did not exist when the child protection laws were passed, it took pride in later years that one of its longest-serving presidents, Absalom Shade Allan, had been directly involved in drafting the first laws designed to prevent the abuse of children. Allan helped draft the original Children's Protection Act of 1892 while serving as the Liberal member for West Wellington in the legislature; and as par-

---

[4] Daily Mercury, Nov. 9, 1893, reports that W. R. Brock, son of Dr. Brock of Guelph, and president of the Toronto Humane Society accompanied Kelso from Toronto to the first organizational meeting. Frank Cooke, in an undated note, states that the younger Brock was from a family resident in Puslinch Township at the time, and after which the Brock Road, south of Clair Road, is named.

[5] 1893 report of Neglected and Dependent Children in Ontario. p 18. Located in the Kelso papers held by the National Archives, Ottawa (MG30, vol. 27).

> **Services offered by The Humane and Children's Aid Society of Guelph City and Wellington County, as outlined on its letterhead, circa 1918:**
>
> ## This Society
>
> Becomes the guardians of dependent and neglected children.
>
> Investigates complains of alleged cruelty to or neglect of children, non-support of families by parent or parents, etc.
>
> Endeavors to preserve the home life by inspiring parents to live better lives, to give up drink and become honorable citizens.
>
> Finds suitable homes for all children committed to its care, and watches over and protects these children after they are placed out.
>
> Attends all trials of children under 16 years of age, in the Police Court, and assists the Magistrate in determining what is best to be done with each case.
>
> Investigates complaints or abuse or ill-treatment of animals.
>
> Carries on extensive educational work among the scholars of public schools for humane treatment of dumb animals.
>
> Is supported, for its aggressive work, almost entirely by voluntary contributions from the public, and your interest and support is earnestly solicited.
>
> One dollar a year and upward constitutes you a member of this society.
>
> All complaints made are treated confidentially. The Society's Inspector will make the investigation.
>
> Report at once all cases of abuse or neglect of children or dumb animals to
>
> AMOS TOVELL, Inspector.

liamentary assistant to provincial secretary Col. J.M. Gibson.[6]

The significance of the 1892 law on the quality of life in this community can't be understated. The law provided the first legal authority for the community to intervene in the lives of families and individuals. It was truly the beginning of a new era, one which held great expectations that attitudes would change and compassion would become an important element in the lives of the dispossessed or the overburdened.

By the end of 1893, there were only five humane societies in Ontario, including Guelph. The child welfare legislation, however, was to act as a catalyst for the organization of societies throughout the province. By the end of 1894, there were 19 humane societies while one year later there were 29.[7] There is, however, some discrepancy in the numbers of humane organizations at the time because Kelso appears to deal solely with the child welfare; his list doesn't include those existing groups that looked after animal welfare. The Toronto Humane Society stated in its 1892 annual report that 21 humane or SPCA groups existed in Canada; nine in Ontario. Peterborough Humane Society, although not included in the THS total for some reason, directed its work solely toward children. This brought the total of all humane and children's aid societies in Ontario to 10.[8]

The 1892 legislation was also the result of continuous efforts by Kelso. He began his humanitarian work as a crusading reporter on the Toronto World newspaper. The newspaper became a tool for him to trumpet humane causes, including one which caused some concern for his employer and competitors: The licensing of street newspaper hawkers, most of whom were young boys. The fact he succeeded and still retained his job as a reporter was a tribute to his ability to convince people of the righteousness of his quest. Before joining the civil service in 1893, Kelso was a founding member and vice-president of the Toronto Humane Society, and helped organize the convention which saw the birth of the Royal Canadian Humane Society in 1892. The Daily Mercury reported in 1903 the Guelph society was started "practically as an off-shoot of the Toronto Humane Society" and the greatest reason for the existence of the Toronto society was "that if something was not done to help neglected children, they would mostly grow up to be criminals." That was precisely the attitude Kelso took in convincing civic and provincial officials of the role humane and children's aid societies could play in the community.[9]

The original Guelph Humane Society constitution called for members to pay a nominal $1 fee each year, subject to the ap-

---

[6] Minutes Nov. 17, 1926, p 374. Clipping from newspaper detailing annual meeting.

[7] 1893, 1894 and 1895 reports of Neglected and Dependent Children in Ontario. The original five societies noted in the annual reports written by J.J. Kelso were: Toronto formed in 1887; London formed in 1891; Ottawa formed in 1882 as the Women's Humane Society (which didn't let men become members until 1900); Peterborough (no date); and Guelph.

[8] Annual report, THS, 1892, p 68. The Ontario humane societies were: Ottawa (formed in 1882); Kingston (no date); Hamilton (1887); St. Catharines (1882); Galt (1890); London (1891); Niagara Falls (1891); Woodstock (1878 as a branch of the Ontario society -- inactive); and Guelph (1893).

[9] Clipping dated 1903 and noted Guelph Mercury. Found in the Frank Cooke papers.

A Century of Caring

Cruelty to animals came in many forms

Cruelty to animals took many forms in the Ontario of 100 years ago. Among the most prevalent were:

The unnecessary and cruel beating of animals

The driving of galled and disabled horses

The overloading of cart horses and teams

The neglect to provide shelter for animals

The clipping of horses, and the docking of their tails

The use of the check-rein and the burr-bit

Matches for cock and dog fighting

Matches for the shooting of pigeons

The clipping of dogs ears and tails

The exposure of uncovered horses in cold weather

The under-feeding and over-driving of horses and cattle

Neglect and cruelty on cattle stock trains

The tying of calves's, sheep's and fowls's legs

The Market Square, located next to City Hall on Carden Street, in 1896. Note the large number of horses, and the board sidewalk in the lower left. This photo was taken from Wilson Street looking east, quite possibly from the tower of the old fire hall which now houses the recreation and parks department.
Photo: Guelph Civic Museum

proval of the board of directors. One presumes approval was necessary because of the sensitive nature of the Society's children's aid role, but there is no report the Society ever turned down a purchased membership. Membership rules, however, allowed for "honorary members (to) be elected in recognition of distinguished services to the society or to the cause of friendless children."[10] There is no reference to distinguished services for animal welfare.

To appreciate how the Society came to be formed, one must understand that the Guelph of 100 years ago was far removed from the city we know today. Guelph in the late 19th century was a community of about 10,500 with wide, unpaved downtown streets[11] alive with the sounds of children, many seeking to make their way in an alien adult world at a very young age, and by the sights and sounds of horses, which formed the basic mode of transportation.

The presence of both the Ontario Agricultural and Ontario Veterinary Colleges, a few miles to the south, made the city an important provincial farming centre. Guelph as a county town was also a centre of agricultural enterprise which drew many farmers to the city.

[10] Article III, Constitution adopted Feb. 6, 1894.
[11] Source: Statistics Canada as reported in Statistical Summary, 1991, a publication of the Department of Planning and Development, City of Guelph.

A Century of Caring

It had two railways that provided easy access for shipping cattle and livestock to the abattoirs of Toronto. And, it was home to the provincial agricultural winter fair long before it moved to Toronto, earning the city world-renown and great prestige by being endowed with the prefix "Royal".

The Guelph of a century ago was a time of "the open market and open barroom" when "men were accustomed to do as they pleased with their horses and cattle. There was much neglect and abuse because of drunkenness of owners."[12]

Concerns over slaughterhouses and stockyards continued for many years into the mid-20th century and beyond. Guelph joined in the efforts of the Canadian Federation of Humane Societies – which it helped to establish – to have parliament pass the Humane Slaughter of Food Animals Act in 1959.

Two young Guelph women (slightly out of focus) take a break on Wyndham Street at one of the Guelph Humane Society fountains installed to provide water for horses. Note the bowl near the curb which was provided for use by dogs and cats.
Photo: Guelph Civic Museum

[12] Typewritten summary of GHS founding, goals and humane activities. Believed dated between 1925 and 1927. Author unknown.

A Century of Caring

But in the early days of the GHS, it was solely the role of animal welfare advocates to change attitudes toward animals through education, example and, in the final instance, by legal means. In 1905, Mrs. Stewart Houston, of Toronto, a speaker attending the GHS annual meeting, called for increased education to end the practice of mutilated trampled animals arriving at slaughterhouses in Toronto.

There was a great need for education in kindness on the farm, Mrs. Houston said. Boys should be taught the proper respect for pets, the habits of animals and the proper use of animals.[13]

Much of the cruelty to horses surrounded their use for delivery and movement of goods. Horses suffered from many abuses, most created by owners who had little concern for the well-being of the animal. Tails, used as brushes to keep insects from bothering them, were docked into "bobs" for a fashionable look; and necks were strained or injured by check reins that were used to hold the animal's head high; or they were simply overworked in an effort to make as many dollars as possible from the energy of the animal.

Society minutes show several resolutions were passed condemning the use of check reins and the docking of tails. These resolutions formed part of the society's continuing efforts to lobby provincial and federal politicians for changes in cruelty laws to outlaw the practices. But, as late as the mid-1960s, the use of check reins and the overloading of sleighs and wagons in Northern Ontario lumber camps continued to raise concerns.[14]

The Society's role during the first half of the past century was devoted to the needs of the city's dog and cat pet population and to the needs of farm horses which brought produce into the city. By 1952, the society maintained six water troughs at locations throughout Guelph, including one outside city hall in what is now John Galt Plaza, for use by farm and delivery animals.[15] These troughs were equipped with municipal water service and automatic faucets which kept the water level high enough for a horse to drink comfortably.

Alcohol abuse was prevalent during the early days of the GHS, so that the Christian virtue of temper-

Demon drink was chief culprit of family abuse

The president can inform the society that there is a good deal of exacting and delicate work in connection with the prevention of cruelty and wrong to children, which is not apparent in the reports and open results. One perplexing phase is the case of families in poor circumstances in which the father occasionally, or frequently, gets drunk, and makes his family more or less a charge on the community. It can hardly be said that such children are exposed to vicious or immoral surroundings, so long as the mother is a decent woman and holds the family together, and yet at times the society feels like giving the children a better chance. In one or two cases, even where the mother's character was a little doubtful it was hoped that the presence of her child or children would save her from further wrong-doing. In a city of our size, the bad cases are not so numerous or so pronounced as in larger cities but yet the society's supervision has extended to a score of families this year, with encouraging results.

Report of the executive committee 1895 annual meeting

---

[13] Minutes, 1905 annual meeting; located in the Family and Children's Services archives.
[14] OSPCA monitored "bush horses", as they were called, as late as the mid-1950s but struggled to keep up with the workload because of a shortage of inspectors and equipment for the northern environs. A bulletin on bush horses issued in June, 1955, notes that "the appalling condition of old bush horses arriving for slaughter in Toronto has been causing us grave concern for sometime." The Guelph society was recognized for its contribution of $50 to the bush horse fund just at a time when the OSPCA was faced with climbing costs. "We're sorry to announce that there is not sufficient money being received to keep pace with the cost of operation, and we may have to discontinue inspections until this fund is more solvent."
[15] GHS minutes, May 6, 1952.

Founding officers of the Guelph Humane Society
Nov. 17, 1893

President:
Lt.-Col. Nathaniel Higinbotham

First Vice-president:
James Goldie

Second Vice-president:
Miss Annie Keating

Managing committee:
Mesdames Thos. Goldie,
J.C. Chadwick, J.C. Keleher,
D. Guthrie, J.D. Freeman,
W.M. Foster, Archdeacon Dixon,
J.C. Smith, R.J. Beattie
and Miss Girdwood;
Messrs. Raymond, Tytler, Bond, Scroggie, Ryan, McElderry, Peterson, Capt. Clark, Mayor Smith and Dr. Brock.

Secretary (pro tem): William Tytler

The appointments of secretary (permanent), treasurer and honorary solicitor were not made until an executive committee meeting on Dec. 8, 1893:

Secretary: Frank W. Galbraith

Treasurer: William Tytler

Hon. Solicitor: A.H. Macdonald, Q.C.

At the Dec. 8 meeting Archdeacon Dixon, Mrs. J.D. Freeman and Mr. Raymond declined appointment to the managing committee. They were replaced by Miss Robertson, Miss Burton, and Mr. Maurice O'Connor.

The society's first inspector was Thomas D. Elliott, appointed in March, 1894.

---

ance was promoted by the Society. This was not just because of the Christian make-up of the society membership, but also because many of its volunteers experienced first hand the misery alcohol inflicted on families. Drink was creating such a problem that by its 1896 annual meeting the Society passed the following resolution:

> *Resolved, that in the opinion of this (executive) committee, it is urgent that some action should be taken by legislation to deal with the misery and cruelty caused by habitual drunkards, and that this legislation should first take the direction of making habitual drunkenness and neglect to maintain a family through this cause a criminal act punishable by imprisonment with hard labor.*

The concern over alcohol and its impact on families and abuse of animals was to become a constant concern. As late as 1916, the director of children's services for Ontario, J.J. Kelso, was expressing concerns but with a new-found optimism that "social reform is moving forward" because "prohibition has removed a great source of unhappiness from so many homes (and) we have much to be thankful for." In hindsight, Kelso's optimism may have been misplaced because alcohol abuse is as much a problem today as it was 100 years ago.[16]

Rev. Amos Tovell, the Society's inspector from 1909 until 1926.
Photo: Guelph Public Library

Christian values were important to the day-to-day work of the society and its decisions. The original bylaws, for example, stated prayer at the opening of meetings was to be conducted at the dis-

---

[16] Letter dated Nov. 22, 1916 to Rev. Amos Tovell from J.J. Kelso.

A Century of Caring

cretion of the chair, but nearly all minutes show prayer was used to open proceedings. Since a member of Guelph's clergy served on the society's executive, or as inspector, almost continuously from 1893 to the mid-1950s, a prayer was most certainly an appropriate opening.

Rev. P.C. Laverton Harris, hired in 1906, formed 72 Bands of Mercy with a membership of 2,063 in his first year.[17] Bands of Mercy were sup-

---

The following item taken from the Daily Mercury of Feb. 19, 1927, is an example of the material provided to Guelph newspapers regularly by the Guelph Humane Society and the Humane Educational League. Commonly referred to as fill copy by the newspaper, this sort of material provided a local source for news or information that would satisfy readers. The practice was gradually discontinued in the late 1960s.

Kindness to All.

Blessed are the merciful for they shall obtain mercy – St. Matthew 5:7

Queen Victoria once said: "No civilization is complete that does not include the dumb and defenseless of God's creatures within the scope of charity and mercy."

The ancient civilizations depending on wealth and force have all perished, and nothing remains but the memory of their former greatness. No nation has survived or ever can survive that exploits the labor of its children or tolerates cruel treatment of dumb animals.

The work, therefore, of our humane societies is much more than a sentimental effort to relieve immediate distress. It is weaving into the warp and woof of our national life those refining and elevating influences that make for national greatness and stability.

Much is being said and written of the necessity of outlawing war, and fortunes have been offered for some practical suggestion for obtaining this much-desired end. But peace will never come to nations through legislation or international law, unless that legislation is the expression of the spirit of love and sympathy in the hearts of the people.

"Man's inhumanity to man, rests on his inhumanity to the lower creatures." The man who beats or ill-treats his horse, will neglect and abuse his wife and child. The boy who is cruel to his pets will grow up to be a menace to society. The record of our penal institutions shows that the most dangerous of criminals are those whose early life was marked by cruelty to helpless animals. The English law goes so far in the recognition of this principle but it does not permit a butcher to serve on a jury when a man is to be tried for his life, on the alleged ground that the butcher's familiarity with the killing of animals tends to make him callous and breeds in him a contempt for human life.

Considered on its lowest plane, humane service is of great value economically. Kindness to animals is a financial asset. It is for this reason that successful packing companies and shippers handling large numbers of live animals value this work done by the Humane Association to prevent abuse and cruel treatment. But the greater assets are in the spiritual values of life. Mercy uplifts the soul and purifies the life. It gives one a sense of kinship with God, for --

"Mercy is an attribute of God Himself and earthly power doth then show likest God's when mercy seasons justice."

By Rev. A.W.S. Garden, rector,
Emmanuel Church, Pittsburgh.
(From a sermon on "The Importance of Kindness to Animals".)

---

[17] Minutes of 1907 meeting located in the Family and Children's Services archives.

ported by the humane movement as early as 1887 "to encourage in every possible way brave, generous, noble and merciful deeds; to protect not only the dependent races, but also every suffering human being that needs and deserves protection."[18] Kelso, who had become a regular visitor at nearly all society annual meetings, endorsed the Bands of Mercy to teach children humane values and to prevent thoughtless cruelty to animals or other children.[19]

The most notable clerical connection with the society is that of Rev. Amos Tovell, a minister of the Disciples of Christ Church on Norwich Street, who served as vice-president and director of the society from 1902-09 and as inspector for the society from 1909 until the separation of the Society into children's aid and humane organizations in 1926.

When Tovell accepted the inspector's post in 1909 he was empowered "as often as he thinks necessary (to) conduct Sabbath services in the towns and villages of the county in aid of the Society's work."[20] Kelso congratulated Tovell for the sacrifice of his ministerial work, expressing the

'Bun' Worton (now Dr. Harold Worton) with Bobby, a horse that was reputed to eat bread as well as sugar. The delivery of goods by horse and wagon was a common sight on city streets into the late 1950s. Harry Worton, who is believed to hold the longest continuous membership in the GHS and operated the family bakery for many years, says it was not unusual for teamsters or wagon drivers to be stopped by members of the Society, and to be reminded to properly care for the animals they used to make a living.

Photo: Alice (Worton) Bayne

[18] pp. 200-201, Aims and Objects of the Toronto Humane Society.
[19] Newspaper clipping of report of annual meeting, 1906. Located in minute book at Family and Children's Services archives.
[20] Special meeting of the executive committee, January, 1909; p 97; GHS minutes located at the Family and Children's Services archives.

A Century of Caring

hope Tovell would "find in your new position many opportunities for the highest kind of Christian service" in helping young people get properly started in life.[21] Efforts were often undertaken to find "Christian homes where (wards and foster children have) a chance to develop and live in surroundings which otherwise would have been impossible for them."[22]

Much of the work of the Society in its early days was undertaken by its membership, partly because the Society's inspector was not a full-time job until 1906 when Rev. P.C. Laverton Harris was hired. This may account for Society board members at times intervening directly in animal welfare cases, disputes involving children and their families, or to offer their homes as a temporary refuge. Authority for the intervention of board members in enforcing the provincial law apparently came from the constitution[23] which gave the management committee the right to appoint its agents. The Children's Protection Act, the only authority given to the society by the province, required no specific local operating structure. But the Act ensured the Society "was given wide, almost unlimited, legal power to apprehend children in all public and private places."[24] This authority gave the society the right to become guardian for a child by simply appearing before a police magistrate, providing some substantiation of its concerns for the child's welfare; and the court would make an order placing the child in a shelter or foster home.

"Besides the work of the inspector detailed in his report," secretary Frank Galbraith writes in the minutes of the 1896 annual meeting, "the ladies of the society and the president have made visits to a number of homes with good results. Several of the chronic cases of last year have removed (sic) from the city, for the present at least, but there is plenty of work with other families."

The presence of a local watchdog on cruelty had a dampening effect on the actions on those who abused children or animals. The Society's members used the authority of the Dominion Cruelty to Animals and Cruelty to Animals in Transit Acts. The cruelty acts provided a $50 maximum fine – a very significant fine in those days – and three months in jail, with or without hard labor, or both.[25]

The initial reaction from the populace to these new laws and the efforts of the individual society members was mixed. Some accepted the principles of the Society's role but occasionally there were people who tested the limits of the law. One person who did test the Guelph Society's rights to intervene on behalf of a child was a mother who organized a few friends to raid the Society's shelter in 1896 and kidnap her son who had been made a ward by the court.

---

[21] Letter dated Jan. 21, 1909 to Rev. Amos Tovell from J.J. Kelso. Kelso's letter indicates there was at least one other clergyman employed in the province at that time as an inspector for a children's aid society in Brantford. Society minutes also note in separate instances that visitors to annual meetings included clergymen from Owen Sound and London who were agents for Children's Aid Societies in their communities.
[22] Report of an interview with Rev. Amos Tovell published in the Guelph Evening Mercury and Advertiser; April 13, 1912.
[23] Constitution adopted Feb. 6, 1894.
[24] Decades of Service, A History of the Ontario Ministry of Community and Social Services: 1930-1980. p 26.
[25] Aims and Objects of the Toronto Humane Society, 1888, p 12. The earliest North American statute on cruelty was passed in British Colonial America in 1641, according to an 1888 report of the Massachusetts SPCA.

This is how the kidnap incident was reported to the 1896 annual meeting by Frank W. Galbraith, of the society's executive committee:[26]

During the past year your society, in its children's aid work, has increased its charges by one, and has now four children under its care.

In the last case, the mother has proven unworthy of the confidence placed in her by your officers when they returned the child after it has been temporarily in their care. Finding that the mother had been drinking, the society a second time took charge of her boy and the magistrate gave it permanent guardianship over the child.

She and her friends, however, did not bow to this disposition of the boy, and made a successful attempt to abduct the him from the shelter. Through the exertions of the inspector, the child was recovered and the parties concerned in the abduction pleaded guilty before the police magistrate and, with the consent of the society, were released on suspended sentence.

The mother of the child was most kindly given another chance by one of the ladies of the society in her own home for some weeks, after which she and her son formed a home together on a farm just outside the city.

Unfortunately, however, last month the misguided mother was induced, presumably by relatives, to run off again with the child and, despite every effort of the society's officers, no definite trace of them was found until last Wednesday when the mother was arrested and put in jail and the child taken to the shelter.

During its first year, the Society operated for little more than seven months with an inspector, yet managed to make 29 inspections, issue 21 warnings, make 16 investigations, take three people to court, two of whom were convicted, had five animals destroyed and arrested two people. But as the knowledge and authority of the society spread, acceptance came about. Thomas Elliott, the society's first inspector reported he was busy during the early months after his appointment in March, 1894, but then saw a gradual decline in the instances of animal abuse.

"These cases of cruelty consist largely of actual violence and injury which hitherto has passed almost unnoticed and also of neglect and carelessness in the attention accorded to the brute creation," Elliott said.[27]

"In the prevention of cruelty to animals, the inspector has been instrumental in cruelty on stock cars, and in having the law governing livestock traffic enforced... (and)... in doing away with animals unfit to work, the society has justified its existence," Galbraith noted.[28]

Elliott's activities were directed to bettering conditions for animals at the stock yards, on the cattle trains and at the fairgrounds. "The cases of violence, maltreatment, and injury to dumb animals are fast disappearing." Elliott noted that his "mild but firm manner" worked in most cases. When a person became obstinate, he escalated his intervention to include

---

[26] Report of the executive committee Third annual meeting Thursday, Oct. 22, 1896
[27] Aims and Objects of the Toronto Humane Society, 1888, p 12.
[28] Minutes of 1894 GHS annual meeting.

a warning; or he charged individuals who were then ordered to appear before Police Magistrate Thomas Saunders.

By 1903 the Society's work was more in the area of child welfare than that of animals. Alderman James Day, city council's appointee to the society, was also arguing that the name be changed to reflect this increasing emphasis on children's protection activities. This was accomplished Nov. 9, 1906, when an annual meeting approved a resolution changing the name to *The Humane and Children's Aid Society of Guelph City and Wellington County*[29]

The impact of the Society on the well-being of animals is difficult to document, given the lack of statistical information.[30] In 1909 only three humane cases were reported to the annual meeting: a farmer who was driving a horse with a sore back; a man from the country spending long hours in a hotel while his horse was left standing tied outside; and a case of pigeon shooting in Elora. Two years later there were 40 reported cases of animal abuse and in 1916, twenty-six cases were investigated.

During its very early days, GHS had rented rooms within homes to provide accommodation for children taken into its care. The first location was on Waterloo Avenue near Gordon Street but as the demand for service increased, it forced GHS to look seriously at constructing its own shelter. This was accomplished in 1911 when Lieutenant-Governor J. M. Gibson officially opened the Society's newly-constructed shelter on Clarke Street. This was the same J. M. Gibson who worked with GHS president A.S. Allan in 1892 to write the first child welfare laws.

The Clarke Street shelter
Source: 1926 annual report

The Clarke Street shelter later became a home for senior citizens operated by the Salvation Army. When the facility closed in 1970, two homes were built on the large lot.[31]

By its 20th anniversary in 1913, the society had grown from a volunteer organization operating on a part-time basis that had taken in two children during its first year to a well-administered and respected children's aid society which operated its own shelter.[32]

Through an oversight at Queen's Park, the Society's name apparently was never actually recorded for official purposes with the Ontario Department of Neglected and Dependent Children. J. J. Kelso, the director of children's services for the province, wrote Rev. Amos Tovell in early April, 1913, saying he "noticed in looking through the records of your society"

---

[29] Letter to J. J. Kelso from Sheriff A. S. Allan, president, and Rev. Amos Tovell, inspector, dated April 10, 1913 Located in Family and Children's Services archives.
[30] Statistics contained in the annual reports dating from the early war years to the separation in 1926 dwelt heavily on child welfare work. Much of the animal humane work, as it was called, was reduced to a general statement or a vague reference to selected cases when reported to annual meetings.
[31] Conversation with Harry Worton, 1991.
[32] After opening in November, 1911, the society's shelter on Clark Street admitted 78 children – 37 from the city, 31 from Wellington County and 10 from outside the county during 1912-13. In addition, the society provided 170 foster homes in Wellington and Halton Counties. Twentieth Report of the Superintendent of Neglected Children, 1913, pp. 58-59.

that it was chartered in 1894 as the Humane Society of Guelph. "I am anxious that your society should be properly recognized as being the (Wellington) county society," wrote Kelso.[33] He instructed Guelph to send him a letter asking for its territory to be extended to cover the county. A postscript added in pen to the typewritten letter, suggests Kelso was aware the charter name had been amended.

Tovell replied a few days later expressing concern the Guelph "society has not been recognized as a county organization." He explained the 1906 change in name and that it had been sent to Kelso for action.

The next mention of the Society's county responsibilities, or concern over its name is recorded as minutes to a special meeting which was held Oct. 29, 1913. During the meeting, a provincial government official stated the authority of the society, with the exception of the original Humane Society of Guelph charter, "was worthless." This created an immediate local crisis because the official also told the Guelph society the province would withhold grants for some children's services because it was not authorized to operate within both Wellington County and the City of Guelph.

A resolution was immediately passed to ask Kelso to "secure a charter for the society operating under the name of ***The Humane Society and Children's Aid Society of the City of Guelph.***"[34] Ninety minutes later at 8:30 p.m., the society executive committee met as "those interested in the organization of a Humane and Children's Aid Society of the County of Wellington." They adopted a resolution calling on Kelso to secure a "charter in the name of ***The Humane and Children's Aid Society of the County of Wellington.***" Less than five weeks later, on Dec. 2, 1913,[35] Kelso informed the society the lieutenant-governor had authorized "***The Children's Aid Society of the City of Guelph in the County of Wellington*** to operate under the authority of the Children's Protection Act."

What prompted the provincial official's comments at that special meeting in 1913 was explained more than a decade later. In a letter to Tovell replying to the Guelph society's concerns in 1926 about the separation of the animal welfare and children's aid responsibilities, Kelso reported that in November, 1913, the lieutenant-governor had given them the official name of ***The Children's Aid Society of Guelph and the County of Wellington*** Clearly, Kelso or his department had failed to act on the 1913 resolutions passed by the GHS and forwarded to his office. The provincial official, Kelso said, who sparked the crisis was acting on "a ruling taken by the provincial auditor and not by any legal authority" when he suggested the Society was acting beyond its mandate. The provincial auditor had claimed that for each municipality there should be a separate and distinct society. "But as you know (this) is not practical. All we ask is that a separate book be kept for wards of the county distinct from the city."[36]

Meanwhile, Kelso told Tovell, the separation of the humane responsibilities would not require any change in name because of the 1913 order-in-council. "You would be quite warranted in leaving out the humane part," he said.

---

[33] Memo to Rev. Amos Tovell from J.J. Kelso dated April 2, 1913. Located in Family and Children's Service archives.
[34] Minutes of special meeting Oct. 29, 1913.
[35] Memo to Rev. Amos Tovell from J.J. Kelso dated Dec. 2, 1913. Located in Family and Children's Services archives.
[36] Letter dated Nov. 25, 1926 from J.J. Kelso to Rev. Amos Tovell. Located in Family and Children's Services archives.

During the First World War a massive dislocation of families and the loss of fathers and husbands to the battles raging in Europe created great demands for service. This was a difficult time for the Society because much of its work was still being conducted with the help of volunteers. By 1915, the Guelph society was involved with 433 children, 67 of whom were placed in the shelter. It also made 31 children wards of the court and placed 33 children in foster homes.[37] The increasing demands for child welfare services were overwhelming, and the desire to keep a constant vigilance on animal cruelty was causing concerns. This difficult period, not just in Guelph but in other Ontario communities, paved the way for the re-establishment of the Ontario Society for the Prevention of Cruelty of Animals in 1919[38] and the movement toward the separation of children's and humane activities became inevitable.

The new OSPCA Act provided a legitimate role for the animal welfare inspector. Not only could the Society destroy an animal – its only legal right until this time – but it could now execute search warrants, seize injured or abused animals, treat them and charge back its expenses to the animal owner. There was now legislation in Ontario that gave animal cruelty inspectors rights to act that were as tough as those under which the children's aid society had been operating for more than 25 years. Federal legislation on cruelty remained in force.

The Society's difficulties in balancing its two roles continued into its third decade as the needs of children continued to escalate with changing times and attitudes. "It appears that we departed from the ways of life, in national, social and personal affairs to such an extent, during the war that we can never return to the olden, quiet, steady ways," said Tovell.[39] The breakdown in traditional values brought on by the aftermath of the First World War caused Tovell to ask the very questions that plague every generation. "One fears for the future when our young people are so anxious for fun, frolic and jazz," he said. "Lawlessness is scarcely considered a disgrace. Immorality is far too common." For more than a decade from the start of the Great War, Tovell had been raising concerns about truancy, minor crime – mostly petty theft – and the acceptance of juvenile labor.[40]

By 1925, one year before the society formally separated, Amos Tovell reported he had been very busy:

> *"We made 1,680 office interviews. We made 248 investigations, having received 169 complaints. We visited 117 children, attended court 100 times, traveled 3,693 miles. Some 678 children were involved during the year."*[41]

In the same year, Tovell told the annual meeting "only a word of caution or advice is usually all that's necessary" to prevent abuse of animals. "It has been necessary," he added, "to have abandoned and homeless animals destroyed – including horses, dogs and cats."

---

[37] Twenty-third Report of the Superintendent of Neglected Children, pp. 54-55.
[38] The Ontario Society for the Prevention of Cruelty to Animals, today's Ontario Humane Society was formed in 1873 but after issuing reports for a few years died because of a lack of funds. The OSPCA was to be reborn in 1919 when the OSPCA Act was passed by the legislature providing powers of arrest and the right to seize and destroy any animal. Source: Aims and Objects of the Toronto Humane Society, 1888; p 9.
[39] Nov. 26, 1925, p 328 Family and Children's Services minute book containing clipping from newspaper.
[40] Tovell had been named truant officer for Guelph in 1909, a post he continued to hold after the society split its functions in 1926.
[41] ibid.

As the needs of the children's aid society grew, there was a growing awareness that education and humane activities were not being fully managed. Education, particularly of animal welfare and the prevention of cruelty, was an important founding principle of the Society. So in late 1924, the Humane Educational League was formed as a sub-committee to promote humane awareness in schools and to promote kindness to animals generally. It's role, conducted by volunteers, could be compared to a similar program offered by the society today which allows the animal shelter mascot and a qualified teacher to visit public and separate schools to discuss humane values and issues surrounding the prevention of cruelty.

Under the leadership of long-time animal welfare Maude Pentelow, the league formed a Junior Humane Society. By the summer of 1926, the Humane Educational League was claiming an enrollment in the junior society of 2,475 children.

The first 'Be Kind to Animals Week' was held in 1925, sponsored by the Humane Educational League to promote the activities of the Junior Humane Society.[42] Children took part in a pet show and a horse parade, both of which "attracted much attention and were considered quite successful."[43] Other league activities included a continued contact with local newspapers to provide material suitable for publication which promoted the goals of the Society.

The GHS's role in the Guelph and Wellington County community was well-established by the mid-1920s and new attitudes had been achieved through diligent hard work. "Conditions are surely much better now," a Society official notes. "Much has been accomplished by legislation and education. Through published articles, public addresses, private interviews and court procedure a new sentiment has been created. New ideals have been established. Only the cruel of heart and the vicious of temper are now suspected of cruelty. The law of kindness prevails, though not quite universally."[44]

As the Society entered 1926 with increasing child welfare demands and a renewed animal welfare mandate being spearheaded by the successful activities of the educational league, Dr. Norman Wallace, president of the Society, and his executive were forced to make a serious decision: hire a second inspector to deal solely with animal cruelty complaints and humane education or to separate the functions of the society.[45] They opted to separate, a decision ratified at the 1926 annual meeting held on Nov. 17 – the 33rd anniversary of the creation of the society. The new Guelph and Wellington County Humane Society dedicated solely to the welfare of animals began formally at its first meeting on Jan. 22, 1927. The new Society would not, however, become incorporated until March 18, 1946, nearly two decades later.

---

[42] The efforts of the Humane Educational League, which was composed of seven women headed by Maude Pentelow, was to play a very significant part in continuing the humane educational activities of the newly formed humane society. On March 1, 1927, the seven members of the league were installed as executive committee members of the new humane society.
[43] Typewritten summary of GHS founding, goals and humane activities. Believed dated between 1925 and 1927. Author unknown.
[44] Ibid.
[45] Report of annual meeting, Nov. 26, 1925. p. 328, society minutes located in Family and Children's Services archives.

"Dog catching is not really part of the work of the humane societies. The only reason that humane societies do this work is that people have confidence that it is done more effectively and humanely than by any other organization. The prevention of cruelty is our real job, and education the most effective way of achieving that object."
Frank H. Cooke,
president, Ontario Society
for the Prevention of Cruelty to Animals
in an address to the Brantford Riding Club
Feb. 17, 1950

A strong leadership

It is important to appreciate that since 1927, when the GHS formally split from the Children's Aid Society, the Society's history is in many ways the story of three individuals: Frank Cooke, Maude Stevenson Pentelow and Sandra Jefferies Bond. These strong-willed individuals each brought to the Society in their time, energy and leadership that helped it overcome adversity – of which there was much because of the constant need to find money to pay operating expenses.

Frank Cooke retired from the Guelph Humane Society in 1973 with a record of service as an executive member of the local society, and various provincial and national agencies that is probably unequaled in Canada or North America. It's unlikely that anyone in Guelph, in all its 166 years has offered as much energy and time to improvement of the community.

"During the mid-1940s at the peak of a busy career in civic organizations, Frank Cooke was actively connected with 12 organizations at one time," wrote the late Verne McIlwraith, veteran civic affairs reporter for the Daily Mercury.[1] Cooke's desire to assist the community was partly the result of the success he achieved in business as a partner in the firm of Cooke and Denison, a machine shop founded in 1923 just four years after he came to Guelph from Birmingham, England.[2]

Frank Cooke, the Society's longest-serving president.
Photo: Mrs. Barbara (Cooke) Wylie

---

[1] Undated "People of Interest" column written by McIlwraith, from the McIlwraith collection of the Guelph Public Library.
[2] Much of the information in this chapter comes from newspaper clippings and interviews given separately to the author and to Eric Colwill by Frank Cooke's widow, the late Nancy Cooke, in 1986.

His commitment to civic affairs was outstanding, and indicative of the devotion and support many GHS members have shown, as noted by the length of service of many of the Society's officers over the years.[3] It's clear from the GHS records, and from newspaper clippings, that Frank Cooke had a businessman's talent for reviving ailing businesses, groups and organizations.

In addition to his humane activities, Frank Cooke's community accomplishments included:

- secretary-treasurer of the Guelph Cemetery Commission for 29 years;

- first chairman of the Guelph Transportation Commission, whose leadership took the public transit service from a deficit (while operating as the former Guelph Radial Railway) to a profit during his 10 years as chairman;

- 11 years as trustee on the Guelph public school board, including one year as chairman;

- president of the Guelph Board of Trade (Chamber of Commerce);

- president of the English Speaking Union;

- a director of the Children's Aid Society;

- first industrial commissioner for the City of Guelph;

- and a supporter of such community groups as the Guelph Little Theatre, Guelph Hunt Club (disbanded in 1935), Guelph Country Club, Kiwanis Club, and the light horse committee of the Royal Agricultural Winter Fair.

Cooke served 44 years with the GHS – 14 years as treasurer and 30 years as president – and 10 years as president and four years as treasurer of the Ontario Society for the Prevention of Cruelty to Animals (Ontario Humane Society)[4]; and was a charter director of the Canadian Federation of Humane Societies, a post he held for 10 years.[5]

"This is not a record but close to it," he wrote Tom Justice, a friend and then-president of the American Humane Association, in 1973.[6]

Cooke began as treasurer of the Society in 1929, the year the first animal shelter was purchased on Waterloo Avenue. In recognition of his efforts, particularly those to revitalize the OSPCA during the early Second World War and early post-war years,[7] Cooke became in 1952 the first Canadian to be awarded the William O. Stillman Medal for "a lifetime of untiring labor for the humane cause and to inspiring leadership in the humane movement."[8]

---

[3] See appendix.
[4] Cooke was the second GHS member to head the OSPCA. Frank K. Baker, who served as president of the OSPCA for one year, immediately preceded Cooke on the provincial society, according to information published for the annual CFHS conference held in Guelph Sept. 21 and 22, 1962.
[5] Letter to Tom Justice, president American Humane Association, dated Feb. 16, 1973, explaining his decision to retire from the GHS board of directors.
[6] ibid.
[7] Letter to Cooke from A. Keith MacLean, OSPCA, dated May 28, 1959.
[8] The citation, presented at a special ceremony in London, Ontario, noted Cooke's service to GHS and OSPCA. It described him as having "in happy proportions the gentle, kindly spirit of the true humanitarian and the wisdom and fighting spirit of a great organizer."

Frank Cooke was the second GHS member to be named president of the OSPCA. Frank Baker, who immediately preceded him as president of the GHS, also held the provincial post immediately prior to Cooke assuming the OSPCA office. When one realizes the OSPCA was not chartered until 1919 – and that Archbishop James Fielding Sweeney, the first president held office for 20 years – it was a rare honor for a small affiliate society like Guelph to be called upon to provide two chief executive officers within the provincial society's first 25 years of service.

The OSPCA also recognized Cooke's efforts in 1954 by conferring on him a Bronze Medal for "devoted and outstanding service to the humane movement in Ontario", an action usually reserved for recognizing heroic acts of bravery by individuals for attempting to save animals from injury or death.[9]

"You've certainly given much of your time and expended a great deal of effort on behalf of the (humane) movement, all of which has been tremendously appreciated," said Mrs. Noel B. Eaton, OSPCA president in 1954. "Where (sic) it not for you, the OSPCA would not exist today, and those of use who are carrying on the work you revived, know this full well, and respect and admire you for all you've done these past years." [10]

But the involvement of the Cooke family in the humane movement didn't stop with Frank Cooke. His wife Nancy was always involved in fundraising activities, whether for the humane society, or for the various other groups with which Cooke was involved. Canon Christopher J. Loat, former pastor of St. James the Apostle Church in Fergus and St. John the Evangelist Church in Elora, who married Cooke's daughter Gladys, served as an executive member of the Guelph society for several years, and as secretary of the OSPCA for several years during the same period that Frank Cooke was president.

Maude Stevenson Pentelow

Maude Pentelow, the daughter of William Stevenson, Guelph's mayor in 1885 and 1886, was a dynamic woman whose love for animals was well-known throughout the community. According to local historian Hazel Mack, Pentelow brought in the most "signed" memberships – "many hundreds" – each year for nearly half a century.

"It is impossible," writes Mack, "to gauge the number of miles Pentelow walked or the number of hours she has given to accomplish her task."

The importance of Pentelow's work, especially the sale of memberships, can't be un-

Maude Pentelow, a tireless worker for the Society.
Photo: Guelph Humane Society

---

[9] Cooke declined to stand for renomination in 1954.
[10] Letter to Frank Cooke from Mrs. Eaton, of Aldershot, Ontario, dated Jan. 27, 1954.

Young geishas participating in the Society's first Be Kind To Animals Week in 1925. No one knows why the young women were dressed as geishas, nor why this photo was taken. The photograph was discovered in an estate lot in 1984 by Guelph antique dealer George Macinnis, who gave it to Susan Porter, a member of the Humane Education Committee.

derstated because the memberships formed a major source of income for the Society during its first half century. Frank Cooke, Maude Pentelow and Sandra Bond have each been successful in bringing together members of the Guelph community who could be called on to assist the society in times of need. Pentelow's efforts, however, went beyond what most people could reasonably expect from a volunteer. Pentelow's fundraising prowess was legendary, the success of which resulted in her being the only person to receive two life membership from the Society: the first in 1923 from the combined children's aid and humane society; and the second in 1949 from the present GHS.[11]

Pentelow's dedication, and desire to raise memberships and funds for the humane cause, continued until her death in 1951. "To the last," noted a resolution passed by the society, "she was working on her membership list when others would have rested."

Slight of stature and filled with a determination rooted in conviction, Pentelow's presence on city streets and at various commercial enterprises often sent shivers down the spine of teamsters and owners of horses which she felt had been abused, overworked or suffered from lack of proper care. Harry Worton, former Guelph mayor, Wellington South MPP and bakery owner, says businessmen in Guelph who used horse-drawn delivery were regularly confronted by Pentelow on city streets.

"She was a very kindly person, always interested in the welfare of animals," says Worton, who has the distinction of holding the society's longest continuous membership, joining as a junior member in 1927. "If the

---

[11] A review of society minutes indicates that Pentelow was the only person awarded a life membership in the society before 1976, when a policy was introduced to make at least one life membership award annually to deserving volunteers.

A Century of Caring

weather turned cold, or it was in the spring and wet weather, I could expect her to call on the telephone and remind me that blankets should be taken along to protect the horses."[12]

Pentelow's formal activity with the humane cause can be traced to 1912 when her name first appears on the Society's executive committee. It is clear that she had already been active in the movement or she would not have been nominated for membership on the Society's most important committee, the one that effectively controlled the day-to-day workings of the Society. The energy she applied to the task of fundraising helped provide for the day-to-day operating expenses, and much of the capital needed to pay for the construction of the Clarke Street children's shelter. Although there appears to be no documented evidence available, it is almost certain that Maude Pentelow's appointment to the executive committee in 1912 was a direct result of her fundraising efforts.

During the years leading up to the separation with the Children's Aid Society, Pentelow was both active and outspoken about animal welfare. She became the spirit behind the formation of the Humane Educational League, a sub-committee of the society formed in 1924 which gave birth to the Junior Humane Society.

The League became "a very powerful and active organization working along the most modern lines," said society president Dr. Norman Wallace.[13] "(S)ince the formation of the Humane Educational League, the work in that department has increased by leaps and bounds." It is easy to see why Wallace made the claim because the League, which sold memberships in addition to the society's general membership, had 450 members.[14] The League membership worked hard "interviewing the public school teachers in order that the children could be enrolled" in the junior society, and in undertaking "garden parties, band concerts and a horse parade."[15]

In addition, "special pictures were brought to the movie houses and there is no doubt that all children were made aware of the 'Be Kind To Animals Week' when it arrived."[16] These special activities were followed by essay contests and the awarding of small cash prizes to children. At the same time the efforts were being made to begin the annual week of celebrations, the women members of the league also embarked on a program of "story-telling to children, both in the schools and the public library, to arouse the sympathy of children in the welfare of animals."[17]

Children from public schools in Guelph, Rockwood joined in the new junior society. The society's objectives sparked interest even from as far away as New Hamburg, west of Kitchener, where 109 children had each paid the five cents required to join the Guelph organization.[18] The junior humane presence in schools outside Guelph gradually diminished but by 1959, the society, which was by now an active sub-committee of the Guelph Humane Society, still claimed an enrollment of 3,082 children, all

---

[12] Interview with author.
[13] Minutes annual meeting, Nov. 26, 1925.
[14] Minutes, annual meeting of Humane Educational League, Feb. 23, 1926.
[15] Undated newspaper clipping believed from the Daily Mercury, undated, believed 1972, headlined Humane Society tackled a big job back in 1893.
[16] ibid.
[17] ibid.
[18] Minutes Humane Educational League, July 20, 1926.

attending city schools.[19] As late as 1971, junior society operated within city schools.[20] Active membership by school children died out by the mid-1970s and was not revived until 1982 when shelter manager Kathy Elliot and Sandra Solomon rekindled the program. By September, 1986, 28 members were enrolled under the leadership of Clover Woods.[21] Unlike the early junior society which involved the enrollment of school children and little direct involvement with society activities, the new junior humane society was organized as a group activity, usually meeting once a month to study or take part in events or activities that promote awareness and concern for animals.[22]

Children who became members of the Junior Humane Society during the 1920s and 1930s received a button, a membership card, a humane picture, admission to a display of animal pictures and a ticket to see the silent film Bell of Atri, a story about how justice was done to an abused and neglected horse. In 1925, to promote the new junior society, all children were invited to take part in a pet show which included a parade down Wyndham Street with their pets.

Pentelow's fundraising accomplishments never waned. Frank Cooke, when he was informed of an illness that kept her from attending a regular monthly meeting, wrote her to express "our very great appreciation for the extra effort you put into the work this year." But more importantly, Cooke noted in his letter of July 7, 1949, that "you'll be glad to know we have enough to practically discharge the mortgage any time, thanks to you."

The mortgage referred to in Cooke's letter was the outstanding balance payable for the construction of the society's shelter on Waterloo Avenue. Pentelow was instrumental in helping the society pay off three mortgages during its lifetime: The first for the children's shelter on Clarke Street built in 1911; the second for the purchase of the Waterloo Avenue property in 1929; and the third for the renovations to the property in 1948 and the construction of what was at the time a very modern animal shelter.

Purchased in 1929 for $3,750 from the Kloepfer family, the Society's first animal shelter at 316 Waterloo Ave. property contained a barn, a house and several acres of land. "At one time a herd of dairy cattle was kept there and a stream ran through the property," said Frank Cooke.[23]

During the height of the Great Depression, when money was scarce and optimism almost as hard to find, Pentelow single-handedly managed to raise funds each year to cover operating expenses and to help pay off the mortgage on the society's first animal shelter.

"Pentelow organized many programs to bring in money for (the mortgage)," said Cooke. [24] "Teas, bridge and finally bingo games, which were then in their infancy, were the principal . . . of money raising."

---

[19] GHS minutes, March 12, 1959.
[20] President's report, 1971 annual general meeting, praising the efforts of Mrs. Howard Bowman.
[21] Minutes of 1987 annual general meeting.
[22] Junior humane took part in the Santa Claus parade every year since 1983.
[23] Ibid.
[24] Undated newspaper clipping circa 1972 headlined 'Humane Society tackled a big job back in 1893'. Believed to be from The Daily Mercury.

Indeed, the success of bingos was so great that Pentelow effectively raised more than two-thirds of the outstanding mortgage of $2,750 during two years (1937-39). The first bingo raised an unheard of $45, a very large amount of money at the time. Encouraged by this success, Pentelow continued with the money-making projects.

It was Pentelow that struck the match that burned the mortgage on the Waterloo Avenue property, an honor bestowed in recognition of her efforts. The Daily Mercury of Feb. 13, 1939, wrote that she described it as "the happiest moment of my life."

On Pentelow's death in 1950 at the age of 79, a resolution passed by the society stated that "it was her efforts alone that enabled the City of Guelph to organize city-wide humane society with a modern animal shelter and a full-time inspector devoted to the care of animals in (Wellington) County." It was a fitting epitaph for a woman who dedicated her life to speaking for those who cannot speak for themselves.

Sandra Jefferies Bond

Sandra Jefferies Bond has been president of the GHS for 11 years of the past two decades. A high energy organizer and an inspired leader, Bond has helped forge a humane society that is not only committed to sustaining its work, but also creating a vision to achieve its goal of preventing cruelty through education and pet ownership responsibility.

Eric Colwill, former city editor of The Daily Mercury, describes her success as having "played no small part in the making of GHS envied throughout Ontario as an organization whose care of, and concern for, animals is expert, efficient and second-to-none." [25]

Born in Bristol, England, Bond's concern for animals came naturally from the adversity of living through the post-war years in a city that had been devastated by bombing. Bristol, a major naval port on England's south coast was a primary military target. Homes were destroyed by the hundreds. Bond collected many of the homeless cats and kittens roaming her neighborhood, fed them and offered them affection.

Later, Bond joined the Royal Society for the Prevention of Cruelty to Animals (RSPCA), the start of what would become a life-long commitment to animal welfare. Today, Sandra Bond lives that commitment by adhering to a vegetarian diet, and refusing to wear clothing made from animals sacrificed for human needs.

Sandra Jefferies Bond, a president with a vision
Photo: The Daily Mercury

---

[25] Printed Pause, newsletter of the Guelph Humane Society, September, 1992.

"It's very difficult but some leathers, for shoes, for example, may be the only exception."[26] She has three cats, and a St. Bernard dog, all of which are pampered and very much loved.

When not serving as president (a role she says she doesn't want to assume again), Bond has been a director, serving at various times as chair of the project and membership committees. Modest about her own contributions, she says "whatever I have contributed has also been, and continues to be, a wonderful learning experience for me."[27] Whenever the question of her contributions to the society are raised, Bond repeatedly points to the individual and collective accomplishments of its members and volunteers. But it is hard not to recognize her personal achievements which include:

- appointment to the dean's advisory committee of the Ontario Veterinary College for two years;

- member for seven years of the Animal Care Committee of the University of Guelph, the first community representative appointed in Canada to an academic research committee responsible for animal welfare;

- member of the University of Guelph's Pet Trust Foundation which oversees research into areas which are designed to benefit animal rather than human needs;

- Chair of the education committee of the Canadian Federation of Humane Societies for three years. During 1992 she served as treasurer;

- and recipient of the Service to Mankind Award presented by the Sertoma Club of Guelph to recognize her unfailing work for the Society, and her genuine respect for all living things.

In 1973, Bond joined with Dr. Ron Downey to take over the helm of the GHS. They placed before a then-inexperienced board of directors a vision that would entail hard work, commitment and money. At the time, through no fault of Frank Cooke who had been constantly seeking new avenues of funding (especially those from municipal sources), the GHS was an organization with few resources, fewer members and a need for greater acceptance and support from within the community.

"I would have fallen by the way-side if we (continued to) run a quasi-pet store," she said, describing her reaction to the society's primary role of dog control during the late 1960s.[28]

Working with Downey, Bond worked to set the GHS on firm financial ground, often – like her predecessor Frank Cooke – using her own financial resources at times to meet pressing bills. Through continued efforts to involve the membership in projects to support the day-to-day operations, Bond succeeded in increasing the numbers of members, and creating a behind-the-scenes crew of dedicated volunteers who continue to provide a significant portion of the annual budget through fundraising ac-

---

[26] Comment to author in an interview, 1992.
[27] Printed Pause, Sept. 1992.
[28] ibid.

tivities. Bond, Downey and the board of directors they helped establish in 1973 can take great pride in that which has been accomplished:

- negotiations with the City of Guelph for the construction of a new pound and animal shelter on municipally-owned lands at the water pollution control plant on Wellington Street in 1974;

- negotiations to resume the animal control contract with the city of Guelph in 1977;

- a spay/neuter program that is central to the Society's goal of reducing the numbers of strays and unwanted animals within the community;

- identification and control programs for cats, thereby helping to return stray cats to owners within the city and as far away as British Columbia, Saskatchewan and Quebec;

- dog obedience classes;

- education programs for new pet owners, special pet needs and visitation to those confined to nursing homes or institutions;

- a humane values program that has been introduced in schools throughout Wellington County, and which is now being studied by other humane societies in Ontario and throughout North America as a model;

- and, reintroduction of the Junior Humane Society, which had died out during the 1970s.

"I will try to be kind to all living things, and will try to protect them, as far as I can, from cruel usage."
Band of Mercy Pledge

Search for an animal shelter begins

Education of humane values, particularly among children, has been a primary goal since before the success of the Bands of Mercy which were started in 1906. However, after Rev. P. C. Laverton Harris left GHS to take up a position with the Toronto Humane Society in 1909, there is little reference in later years to the continued operation of the Bands.

The Junior Humane Society was formed in 1925 and it became the new focus within the community to educate and to develop a public compassion for animal welfare. During the years after 1927, educational programs, although still very much at the centre of the Society's efforts, failed to expand much beyond the school classroom because of the Great Depression. GHS had a major burden just carrying out day-to-day operations. And, later, as the Depression eased, a world war and a continuous period of civic growth placed added stress on its ability to provide little more than animal control services.

The immediate need following the separation with the Guelph Children's Aid Society was for an animal shelter. This need had been identified in 1925 by the Humane Educational League but the priority then had been toward child care needs. The first shelter opened by the Society in 1911 was designed solely as a child care facility. The only animal presence in the very first shelter was that of a pet or mascot which helped pro-

The first animal shelter was built on this property at 316 Waterloo Ave. in 1948. Although the property was purchased in 1929, it was not until 1948 that a contemporary shelter building, seen at rear, was constructed. Prior to 1948, the society housed animals in a barn on the property. This photo was taken by the author in 1992.

A Century of Caring

vide a home-like environment.

It wasn't until 1929 that the first animal shelter was opened. Several sites had been proposed: a Waterloo Avenue property which would eventually be purchased, and others on Elora Road, Woolwich Street, Exhibition Street, Perth Street; and Oxford Street.

After considerable discussion, in part because of the availability of a barn on the property to act as a temporary shelter, the board of directors decided on April 9, 1929, that a committee be struck to close a deal, for the property at 316 Waterloo Ave. The GHS, which had been given $500 in seed money when it separated from the Children's Aid Society two years before, now had about $1,800 with which to purchase the land. But a close inspection of the property by the committee showed it needed repairs to the house and the barn needed to be rebuilt. The decision to purchase was delayed while the executive committee looked for a more suitable property.

By April 29, 1929, the society "could not come to an agreement about (whether to purchase) the (Waterloo) Avenue property," the minutes show.[1] The next preferred location appeared to be a house at 515 Elora Rd. Although the home was in good repair and located next to a lumber yard and the railway, it was much too expensive. The minutes report that a member of the executive committee was to meet with the owner to discuss a reduction in the asking price because "$8,000 was out of the question." The owner refused, and the society began to look – again – at the Waterloo Avenue property.

Finally, a Mr. Wilson of the Toronto Humane Society looked at the Waterloo Avenue property. "He said it was ideal in every way," reported the minutes of a May 13, 1929 meeting. "Mrs. Pentelow had also seen various tradesmen who would devote (sic) paint, paper, etc. The porch and shingling would cost only $250."[2] A decision to purchase the property was carried at the May 13 meeting. Within a month, the society moved onto the property, described as "ideal as it had a large amount of land, a solid brick house, a good bank barn and a fine spring." Cost was $3,750, of which $2,750 was carried as a mortgage.

Although the barn was renovated and was to be used only as a temporary shelter, it provided service for nearly 20 years because of economic necessity. Less than six months after the shelter property was purchased, all capital fundraising plans were displaced by the onset of the Great Depression. For the next decade, all fundraising was devoted to raising money to pay the inspector, satisfy daily operational needs and to meet the mortgage payments.

The Waterloo Avenue property purchase, whether by luck or design, was a far-sighted move by the Society. It provided a sound in-

---

From the Daily Mercury, May 14, 1929

HUMANE SOCIETY IS BUSY ORGANIZATION

The monthly meeting of the Humane Society was held on Monday afternoon with the following members present: Dr. Fowler, Mrs. Pentelow, Miss Graesser, Mr. Laidlaw, Mrs. Cooke, Miss Allan, Mrs. Baker, Mrs. Hewer, Mrs. Johnson, Mrs. Wells, Mr. Hicks, Mr. Fraser. Inspector Fraser's report for April showed that there had been 30 calls, 15 investigations and seven warnings. One dog and four cats were humanely destroyed, two dogs were placed in homes. First aid was rendered on two occasions to dogs in accidents. A dog that had been in a motor accident two months ago had practically lost the use of its hindquarters. The owner was advised to have it destroyed. The owner of a Victoria Road dog was found. A sick pet canary was humanely destroyed. On a farm near New Germany animals were found to be in a dreadful condition, as they were being fed hay not fit for bedding. A letter was written to Kitchener advising them to prosecute. Horses needing medical attention were ordered to a veterinary. A number of owners were ordered to drive their horses more carefully, or to take better care of them. Several delegates from Guelph will attend the convention held by the Toronto Humane Society on May 17th. Among them are Dr. Fowler, Mr. Fraser, who will give a report of the Guelph society, Mrs. Pentelow, Mrs. Hewer, Mrs. F. K. Baker and Mrs. Gordon Johnson.

---

[1] GHS Minutes, April 29, 1929.
[2] ibid.

vestment in the future by allowing the GHS to offset the devastating financial effects of the Great Depression by severing building lots on Waterloo Avenue and on Webster Street (now known as Bristol Street) at the rear of the property.

The society has faced a continual struggle to maintain its finances and to pay its bills. When it was established in 1893, the society boasted a first year of operation on $51. However, $10 of that first revenue was from one person who purchased a long-term membership. By 1895, GHS faced the need to ask city council for a grant. A $50 grant in 1896, used primarily for its child welfare activities, was the first of annual grants from city council which recognized the contribution provided by the Society. This grant, which was never enough to sustain the operation, continued after the separation from the children's services organization.

During this same period, the instances of cruelty began to decline in proportion to the use of horses for commercial delivery. There is very little recorded about specific cases of cruelty during this period, but many letters were received from people with complaints about the care of pets by neighbors.[3]

By late 1947, the barn that had acted as shelter for nearly two decades was in desperate need of repair. Cooke called the situation a crisis without precedent for the city and the society.[4]

"The shelter or barn which has been temporarily in use for many years is obsolete and reflects no credit on the humane society or the City of Guelph," said Cooke.[5] "It has moved off its foundations which are themselves buckled and shaky and cost of repairs or conversion would not prove economically sound, owing to its size and structure."

The society proposed a fully-equipped shelter at the same location – 316 Waterloo Ave. – which was then still officially a property within Guelph Township. But efforts to get the project started became almost immediately stalled by a decision of the city solicitor that grant money for a humane society capital project could not be made by city council.

GHS, which had been acting in good faith as unofficial dog catcher for the city since 1935, had received an $800 annual grant which represented in reality "only 30 per cent of expenditures (while) dog-catching and enforcement requires 90 per cent of our effort," Cooke said. The Society sought a $2,600 grant from the city to make up the difference between the $2,400 it had in reserve for the project and the estimated $5,000 construction cost.

This situation led to a unique solution, one that placed both the City of Guelph and the (then) Guelph and Wellington County Humane Society in the forefront of the Canadian humane movement: the society, for the sum of $3,000 annually, was to become the official poundkeeper for the municipality, the first time in Canada that a humane society had been contracted for municipal animal control services.[6]

---

[3] An undated and unsigned note containing statistics for the 1947 annual report state that during 1946, this type of complaint resulted in 34 investigations, all of which proved to be unfounded.
[4] Letter to city council from Cooke dated Nov. 13, 1947.
[5] ibid.
[6] Comment by Rev. Christopher Loat, secretary of the Ontario SPCA, to the annual meeting of the GHS, Jan. 26, 1948.

The decision, however, wasn't totally unanimous. Ald. A.J. Frank remarked at the council meeting Jan. 20, 1948, it wasn't a good deal.

"We didn't strike a good bargain, then, through this legal angle, if we're going to pay $3,000 a year." The 'legal angle' that Ald. Frank referred to was a second attempt by city council in late 1947 to approve a loan to the society to construct the shelter. City councillors were told such a loan was illegal, so efforts were made to find a way to provide financial assistance while at the same time remaining within the authority of the Ontario Municipal Act.

In a letter to the department of municipal affairs on Oct. 21, 1947, city solicitor R. Stewart Clark wrote that a loan was clearly illegal under the Ontario Municipal Act, "nor has (council) the power to turn over the revenue from the dog tax." R. L. Kennedy, a supervisor in the department replied Oct. 28, 1947, stating that under the Dog Tax and Livestock Protection Act the city had the authority to grant money for the operation of the pound and the services of a dogcatcher."

In the end, the city struck a deal with the society to provide the services of an inspector and a truck – the first ambulance purchased by the society. In return, taxpayers paid for animal control services but city council did not make an annual grant to the society to cover its humane activities.[7]

While this deal didn't sit well with a few people, those that defended it did so with vigor: "The society gets little thanks and little help in their work. There is always some technicality to stop us from helping them out," said Ald. Douglas Keefe.[8] He viewed the contract as a chance to help put the society back on a firm financial footing. It didn't, however, keep the society from holding a mortgage on the property. At the 1948 annual meeting, Frank Cooke noted that only $1,500 – 50 per cent of the annual contract – had been paid so far. That necessitated a five-year loan of $3,000 from the Ontario Society for the Prevention of Cruelty to Animals (OSPCA) to help the Guelph society overcome its immediate financial needs.

Keefe's remarks were based partly on the success of efforts by the Society to sell dog tags during 1947. Sales of tags were conducted through the police department, but the society undertook in 1947 to check on the numbers of tags being issued, and to see that all dogs had tags, said Ald. F.L. Freudeman.[9] Keefe declared that "the society took an interest in things" and that as a result taxes had been lower for citizens of the city. During 1947, the society collected $4,482.50 in dog tag, more than $1,300 more than the $3,132.40 that had been collected in 1946.[10] To this, Ald. Freudeman added that "it's well-known that up to now about two-thirds of the dogs in Guelph don't have tags."[11]

---

[7] The Daily Mercury of Jan. 21, 1948, reports: "Under the present bylaw, council's desire to aid the society in its work has been accomplished – legally, the city will establish an animal pound as required under the Municipal Act." Frank Cooke notes in his papers that a poll was conducted among Guelph residents in 1948 asking whether city council should support the humane society. According to Cooke, the results were very highly in favor of support for the society. Details of the poll – when, where and what question was asked – have not been located.
[8] Daily Mercury, Jan. 21, 1948.
[9] ibid.
[10] ibid.
[11] ibid. That figure remains true today.

Insp. Len Shaw with the society's first ambulance, a van purchased in 1948 to carry out animal control duties for the City of Guelph.

Photo: Guelph Public Library, Vorn McIlwraith Collection

GHS opened its second animal shelter in 1948, a planned contemporary structure that still exists behind the home at 316 Waterloo Ave. The success of both capturing the municipal dog control contract, with its requirement for a vehicle, and the construction of a new shelter gave the Society's inspector increased credibility and importance in the community.

Until this time, the inspector had to do his best catching dogs and housing animals in the barn. If the barn was full, the inspector housed dogs in his own residence, or in homes of friends of the Society. Prior to the municipal contract being awarded to GHS, it was also common to see the Society's inspector attempting to go about his business on foot.[12]

"Now we don't have to feel ashamed, as we used to, to see our inspector walking around with a sack over his shoulder," said Frank Cooke, announcing that the society had purchased its first animal ambulance at a cost of $1,487. The truck, equipped with cages and equipment to assist injured animals, represented nearly all of the $1,613.11 deficit reported for the society at the 1948 annual meeting.

During the post war years, the Guelph Humane Society settled into its role as dogcatcher for the city, and agents for the OSPCA. Educational efforts continued with annual enrollments of school children in the Junior Humane Society.

---

[12] Daily Mercury, Jan. 27, 1948.

A Century of Caring

"If thy heart be right then will every creature be to thee a mirror of life and a book of holy doctrine."
Thomas a Kempis (A.D. 1380-1471)

Pressure for change

The need for a new shelter continued to build during the early 1960s. As neighborhood growth became more residential around the shelter on Waterloo Avenue, complaints became more frequent, often involving deputations to city council by angry residents who demanded the shelter be moved outside city limits.[1] The irony was that the shelter had been outside the city limits when it was first purchased in 1929.[2]

The problem of noise from the kennels would eventually cause a rift between city politicians and the Society, which resulted in the society ending its contract to provide animal control and poundkeeping services. It would terminate a relationship that had begun in 1935 when the GHS accepted an invitation to monitor the sale of dog tags.[3] The controversy over barking at the Waterloo Avenue shelter would also play a part in Guelph Humane Society severing its affiliation with the Ontario Society for the Prevention of Cruelty to Animals (OSPCA), or as it is more commonly known, the Ontario Humane Society.

As the society moved into the 1960s, public awareness of humane issues began to build quickly. GHS, through its membership in the Canadian Federation of Humane Societies, was basking in the success of finally getting Parliament in 1959 to pass new regulations that cleaned up the meat packing industry and imposed humane controls on the slaughter of livestock.

As the decade progressed, there were numerous groups throughout the world working to raise awareness of animal rights and seeking to ban the seal hunt on Canada's east coast. Others, especially those in Europe, were seeking to ban trapping of fur bearing animals. The Society played a role in these issues by passing resolutions in support of actions taken by the OSPCA and the CFHS, to help fund research studies of the issues, send observers to the seal hunt and to assist in the development of humane traps.

As early as 1961, Frank Cooke was writing politicians trying to get action to stop what he described as the "horrible cruelty and wanton destruction of seals in the seas off Newfoundland."[4] Cooke condemned the practice of indiscriminate shooting of seals that were killed or wounded from long distance, only to be abandoned and left to die on the ice floes.

---

[1] Letter, Sept. 11, 1962, to F.H. Cooke from Mildred Tovell, city clerk, requesting meeting with finance committee to discuss a petition from shelter neighbors.
[2] Guelph's population in 1967 was 52,161. Source: City of Guelph planning department.
[3] Letter, July 19, 1968, to city council from F.H. Cooke. Guelph Humane had accepted an invitation from city council in 1935 to control the sale of dog licenses in the city. No formal agreement existed for payment for services but the society received an annual grant that helped offset the cost of animal control services, which included the employment of an inspector.
[4] Letter to J. Angus MacLean, Fisheries Minister, House of Commons, Ottawa, dated Jan. 23, 1961. MacLean expressed platitudes about being concerned about the decrease in the harp seal stocks off the East Coast but declined to assure Cooke that anything would be done until " the hunting methods used in the industry were reviewed in order to be sure that the most humane methods possible are being used."

"This is a sad economic picture of conservation practices," Cooke wrote, "representing as it does a tremendous loss of our natural resources."

Guelph also supported the Canadian federation's sponsorship of humane trapping research at McMaster University and the University of Guelph. Funded through grants to the Canadian Association for Humane Trapping and the Association for the Protection of Fur Bearing Animals, this research was considered "the first project for this purpose ever undertaken in Canada and as far as we know in any other country," said Judge J. deN. Kennedy, a past president of the CFHS.[5]

Frank Cooke called on city hall in 1965 to increase the level of financial assistance offered GHS in its role as the municipal animal control service.

"There should be two dog control officers," Cooke wrote Mayor Ralph Smith. "It is quite impossible to cover the city with one man in the daylight hours."[6] This inability to patrol the entire city was a result of Guelph's significant growth both in population and in area.

With this population growth, Cooke said, also came the need to increase the size of the shelter. He proposed a new shelter at the rear of the Waterloo Avenue facility, fronting on Webster Street (now Bristol Street). Urban development had come to the area which, in 1929 when the shelter first opened, was little more than a small farm just outside the city limits.

For years, Cooke had been seeking a contract that represented the true cost of providing the municipal dog control service. The civic underfunding generally had been offset by charitable contributions made by supporters of the Society. On April 12, 1966, Frank Cooke met with the city's finance committee to discuss the on-going financial problems and needs.[7] But little was resolved other than to have the city ask Cooke and the society to detail their needs in a letter to a committee.

A cost-conscious council, however, refused to look at various proposals which included the hiring of additional staff or the need for a two-way radio[8] to improve service of citizen complaints. During the mid-1960s, the operation of animal control was based on a method of patrolling the city and having the inspector stop regularly and telephone the shelter for messages. In late 1964, a telephone answering service was hired but within four months the cost was found to be too expensive and it was cancelled.[9]

The city's concern about the Society's role in Wellington County also brought into focus concerns Cooke was having about the lack of grants it received from county politicians during the previous three years. On June 1, the Society formally asked for a change in name to *Guelph Humane Society, Inc.* and turned over humane services within Wellington County

---

[5] Letter to Frank Cooke dated Oct. 2, 1970, in which Kennedy outlined the start of a four or five year project costing the federation as much as $50,000 in grant money.
[6] Letter, Jan. 11, 1965, to Mayor Ralph Smith from F. H. Cooke.
[7] Letter to Cooke from Mildred Tovell, city clerk, dated April 13, 1966.
[8] Letter to city clerk Mildred Tovell from Cooke dated May 12, 1966, set the cost of the radio at $2,439.35. Tovell responded June 14 stating that finance committee "recognized the need but felt the cost was too much when provision was not made in the 1966 estimates.
[9] In a letter to the finance committee dated Feb. 8, 1966, F.H. Cooke notes that a request for a $6,000 grant in 1965 was reduced to $5,000 by the committee, resulting in a **$807.35** deficit on operations. "It's respectfully requested that this request for $6,000 for 1966 receive your serious attention," he wrote. Two years before on Feb. 7, 1964, Cooke wrote the committee that its annual $4,500 grant had not risen since 1956. As a result, he notes, the society had a deficit of $477.21 in 1962; $1,317.52 in 1961; and $1,402.81 in 1960. One area of concern by city officials was the cost of society services to Wellington County. In a letter to city clerk Mildred Tovell date May 12, 1966, Cooke noted that in 1965 the society provided services valued at $675 to the county. These services were the result of referrals from OPP officers, often requiring the services of a veterinarian. "This is strictly a service to the county as we act as a law enforcement agency," Cooke noted. The next year the society re-organized, dropping its connection with the county after no funding grants were made.

to the Ontario Humane Society. The letters patent was approved Nov. 18, 1966, 73 years and one day after the society was founded under the same name.

Meanwhile, city council was still pushing for resolution of the problem of barking dogs. To avoid getting itself into the same situation again, city council proposed in its 1966 dog licensing bylaw that, among other revisions which prevented ownership of more than two dogs and two cats, no "dogs or cats are housed or kept in a separate building located not closer than 40 feet from any dwelling or building where persons congregate, meet or work."[10]

"There is no legislation to prevent dogs barking in the daytime, and as you know we must keep strays for 72 hours," Frank Cooke wrote city council."Please be assured that everything possible is being done to keep the shelter as quiet as possible."[11]

By 1967, the society was actively looking at options and sites available within the city for a new shelter. A tentative site favored by the executive was located where the present shelter stands – on two acres of land at the water pollution control plant on Wellington Street.[12] The estimated $40,000 cost of the facility could be paid for from a mortgage and from a $15,000 contribution from the society and a tentative offer (included in the budget estimates for 1967) of a contribution of $15,000 from the city.[13]

The question of a home for the poundkeeper and inspector also became an important issue related to a location on Speedvale Avenue west near Imperial Road where city council planned a water well, sand storage, water tower and fire station. The Society was concerned that the sale of the shelter at 316 Waterloo Ave., also used as a residence for the society's inspector, would raise its monthly operating costs by an estimated $125 because of the loss of the inspector's housing benefit. Council ultimately rejected any proposal for a residence on the industrial-zoned property. They did, however, build a water tower and a water well on the property. The city still retains plans to build a fire station at that location.[14]

Frank Cooke expressed concern that since city council had only planned on matching the $15,000 provided by the Society, there was a question of how the relocation funding would be covered.[15] Another difficulty was that the Speedvale Avenue location was too far removed from the city proper which would prevent "citizens and particularly young people to visit and partake of activities at the shelter." The society countered with its 1965 proposal to build a new shelter at the rear of its own property which fronted on Bristol Street. Cooke suggested the Bristol Street shelter proposal could be built with noise controls in place to eliminate ongoing complaints about barking dogs from nearby residents.

---

[10] Attachment to letter of April 13, 1966, to Frank Cooke from city clerk.
[11] Letter to city council from Frank Cooke dated July 19, 1968
[12] Letter, Feb. 5, 1967, to city clerk Gordon Hall from F.H. Cooke. Architect Karl Briestensky, engaged in late 1966 by the society, also endorsed the use of the sewage treatment plant site.
[13] Ibid.
[14] Although the references in correspondence relate to a location on Speedvale Avenue, a photocopied subdivision plan included with the Frank Cooke papers shows a 1.2 acre site proposed for the humane society on a new street (assumed to be Imperial Road because it is one block west of Royal Road) which runs north from Speedvale. The site plan shows a water tower (which does exist today on the site), sand storage and a lot designated "other uses. A fire station is located on a corner lot which appears to be the present location of the Gideon's International building.
[15] Letter, April 7, 1967, to Ald. Chris Robinson from F. H. Cooke.

Part of the concern over the Speedvale property was money. The Society had been fighting an accumulating deficit on operations for several years, so it was elated when city council responded positively to the Bristol Street proposal by calling on the building inspector to prepare sketch plans for an animal shelter in collaboration with society officials.[16] This was a short-lived proposal, however, as council reversed its endorsement of enclosed dog runs a few months later and ordered "the shelter should be relocated away from residential development."[17]

City council had at the same time been consulting with the Ontario Veterinary College about the use of its facilities to hold dogs picked up within the city. This was an action that would become a wild card in negotiations taking place between GHS, OSPCA and council in late 1968.

It wasn't until this time, however, that any serious attempt was made toward resolving the question of a new shelter. City council formed a special committee on dog control in May which called on the GHS and Ontario Humane to provide animal control contract costs. Although there was no submission before the fall sittings of council, the decision in the spring set the stage for the end of the Guelph society's mandate for animal control at the end of the year.

When the committee reported to council in September it called for invited tenders from OSPCA and the GHS for the operation of the city's dog control program.

This decision was a severe blow to the GHS because it widened a recent rift between the two societies. Guelph had been a founding member and strong supporter since the OSPCA was chartered in 1919 but a dispute over the management and operation of the Guelph shelter had surfaced earlier that summer. Particularly upsetting was the recognition that city council was prepared to act on an offer from OSPCA to provide animal control services, and to construct a new animal shelter at OSPCA expense while at the same time it operated a humane society in the city in competition with the Guelph Humane Society.

Cooke charged that OSPCA general manager Tom Hughes "has encroached on the territory of an affiliate society, offering to build a pound for the City of Guelph and to start a new humane society."[18] This was supported by The Daily Mercury which reported on May 24, 1968, that Hughes had "been critical both of the local shelter and the method of operation here" and suggested the best animal control service was "an efficient, active, virile humane society;" namely the OSPCA.

More importantly, a letter from the city told GHS in very blunt terms it wanted the Waterloo Avenue shelter moved. There was no suggestion the city was prepared to assist financially in its relocation. Ald. Pat Hanlon, chairman of the special dog control committee, suggested the society purchase city-owned industrial property for the new shelter at market value of $6,000 an acre.[19] Hanlon's letter followed three meetings in Au-

---

[16] Letter, June 27, 1967, to F.M. Woods, city administrator, from W.G. Hall, city clerk.
[17] Letter, Nov. 7, 1967, to F. M. Woods, city administrator, from W.G. Hall, city clerk.
[18] Copy of letter dated Oct. 21, 1968, to Basil Capes, president of Ontario Humane from Frank Cooke. Cooke chastised the provincial society for reversing its philosophical position on dog control. Cooke viewed dog control as an extension of humane operations, a view not shared by Ontario Humane during the early 1960s. "Now (Tom) Hughes has completely turned around and is willing to spend money (collected for anti-cruelty) on building dog pounds for municipalities. It is alright for a humane society to do dog control but the building of pounds is the responsibility of the municipality," Cooke said.

A Century of Caring

gust and September at which "we were regaled with the present high cost of dog control and the number of complaints," Cooke said.[20] The committee decision also seemed to reject an earlier decision in which Aldermen Pat Hanlon, Hayes Murphy and Chris Robinson were ordered to "proceed with the preparation of plans and specifications for the construction of a small animal shelter and pound" and to continue negotiating with GHS.[21]

Within a week of the committee decision, GHS announced its intention to end the animal control contract. "The society is willing to have the city relocate a satisfactory shelter, but it must be the city's expense and on a permanent basis," Cooke wrote city council.[22] "It is the desire of the humane society to improve its shelter (on) Waterloo Avenue by closing in its runs, providing new cages and generally removing the alleged cause of complaints which are said to have arisen." Council immediately called on the society to reconsider its decision and one month later negotiations were active in attempting to reach a compromise.

The society's lawyer, William Hamilton, who entered the negotiations as a mediator proposed three options to the city [23] that seemed suitable to city hall. He urged Cooke to respond favorably to the concerns raised by council which sought a "business-like proposal" with a breakdown of the costs of both the city and the society operations, a breakdown on construction costs and an amortization schedule. "After speaking with Ald. (Hayes) Murphy, we were quite reassured that it was not the intention of the city council to give the Guelph Humane Society the runaround and that they will make every effort to negotiate some satisfactory agreement with the society for the continued operation of the dog control requirements of the city," Hamilton said.

In addition, Hamilton said, it appears council wants "some alternative proposals whether to put one dog control officer on or two, whether you are providing service for eight hours a day or 12 hours a day or 24 hours a day and the various cost factors involved." And that's where talks broke down. Cooke responded by suggesting that instead of the city's present one-man, one vehicle operation costing about $8,500 a year, the city should operate a service with three men and two vehicles, at a cost of $22,380 a year.[24]

The demand for an expansion of 'adequate' service was also consistent with the view Cooke had about dog control being an extension of humane projects. "It has been established that 50 per cent of all dogs running at large or either killed or injured," the Daily Mercury reported in a story about the 1968 annual meeting.[25] The same story quoted Cooke as saying dog control has not been keeping up with the growth of the city. Cooke's views, however, may have clouded the now-deteriorating negotiations

---

[19] Ald. Pat Hanlon, chairman of the special committee, said in a letter dated Sept. 20, 1968, to the society that the Waterloo Avenue shelter would have to be relocated; the society should own its own land and building used for the city pound; and GHS was free to negotiate the purchase of a two-thirds of an acre unserviced lot reserved for it in the northwest industrial basin. Cost was set at $3,900. Hanlon noted in his letter "city council are (sic) desirous of having an effective enforcement of the dog control regulations under a system which will ensure good value and service on a continuing basis related to the money expended."

[20] Undated, unsigned copy of letter from the Guelph Humane Society (F.H. Cooke) to Mayor Paul Mercer. The letter, outlining the society's position in ending its contract for dog control, was quoted in part by The Daily Mercury on Oct. 22. Cooke noted the cost of animal control for 1967 was $6,157, or $513 a month, while in 1968 the cost was expected to reach $8,436, or $703 a month.

[21] ibid. In his letter, Cooke notes that a Sept. 18 meeting "reiterated the objectives previously reported but did not touch on the agenda, which was to proceed with the plans and specifications of a new shelter."

[22] Letter, dated Sept. 26, 1968, from F. H. Cooke.

[23] Letter dated Nov. 20, 1968 to F. H. Cooke.

[24] Letter, dated Nov. 28, 1968, also proposed a 2,500 square foot shelter to be built on identified city land, graded and serviced, and turned over to the society for the sum of $1. The letter included an operations budget based on a $30,000 shelter built on land supplied by the city. The $22,380 budget was based on a per capita cost of 42 cents for each of the city's 53,300 residents.

[25] Guelph Daily Mercury, May 10, 1968.

with city council which appeared to have problems differentiating between the humane and dog control roles of the society.[26]

Cooke summed up the GHS efforts to sort out the 1968 negotiations for the animal control contract as "a trying year." The Society was "held up to ridicule" and when the city pressed for the GHS to reconsider its decision to end the contract, "we should not have listened to them."[27]

The Society's operation of the city animal control services ended on Dec. 31, 1968. The next day the Guelph Animal Hospital, owned by Dr. Norman Hawkins, a member of the society's board of directors, began to operate Guelph's civic pound services. The city public works department took over the role of dog catcher.[28]

The irony is that the city, which thought it could save money by taking over the animal control services after the society ended the contract in 1968, ended up spending almost as much money in 1969 as Frank Cooke predicted was needed to provide a proper three-person service for the city. And the city did this while only using one city employee who did not work beyond 4 p.m. each day, or on weekends. The Daily Mercury reported[29] that in 1969 the city spent $21,169 to provide less service to the citizens of Guelph than the society had provided during any of the previous 20 years it held the contract. The deficit on operations was $9,356, nearly $900 more than the total the city paid the humane society for its animal control in 1968. The financial picture for 1970 was better but the cost of animal control was $17,614, including a deficit of $1,389.

By early 1969, the Society was getting desperate for a new shelter, but having abandoned its role as poundkeeper for Guelph, city council was not prepared to provide substantial financial assistance. GHS made[30] a request to purchase a property on Lewis Road in the city's new northwest industrial area for the sum of one dollar. When finance committee met in April, it rejected the request although during the previous summer, city council had authorized the reserving of property in the industrial area for an animal shelter and dog pound. The decision came less than a month after the city's finance committee also rejected a grant for the society.[31] Financial pressures were exacerbated by changes in labor laws which required the society to end the informal arrangement it had with its inspector to work a regular work week but remain on call 24 hours a day seven days a week. In his 1969 annual meeting report, Cooke noted that a "kennel maid" had been hired to relieve the inspector's work-related responsibilities.

Then council, in a vote that signed the death warrant for many abandoned dogs, refused a request fundamental to the philosophy of all humane societies – that stray dogs be given every opportunity to be

---

[26] Undated, unsigned letter from Guelph Humane Society (F.H. Cooke) to Mayor Paul Mercer. "Donations made to this society are for the prevention of cruelty to animals and must be used for humane purposes. To buy land and erect a pound which it is the function of the city to supply is clearly a misuse of funds entrusted to it." The letter, however, was referred to and quoted in part in a Daily Mercury story on Oct. 22, 1968. Ald. Ken Hammill "felt Cooke's letter was a 'slap on the wrist which we deserve'," the Mercury story reported. It is clear from Cooke's letter that negotiations had reached an impasse with a loss of respect and trust by each of the parties. Cooke called for no more involvement by the society in offering to continue its services in 1969. Cooke wrote: "He (Cooke) has to his credit the longest years of service in the entire civic structure, having served continuously since 1926 progressively on the school board, transportation commission, children's aid society, the cemetery commission and the Guelph Humane Society. His length of service demands respect and his opinions should be valued." The Mercury story on Oct. 22 also summed up the position of many council members when it stated Ald. F. W. Dixon "declared that the work of the society was excellent in humane work but there had been little in dog control."
[27] President's report, 1969 annual meeting
[28] Notice attached to letter to society dated Dec. 27, 1968, from F.M. Woods, city administrator.
[29] Undated Daily Mercury clipping found among the Frank Cooke papers headlined 'No dogs destroyed by city reflects new canine law'. Believed published early 1971.
[30] Letter, Jan. 9, 1969, to F.M.Woods, city administrator from W.G. Hall, city clerk
[31] Letter to Frank Cooke from city treasurer Milt Sather dated March 18, 1969.

reclaimed or adopted before being destroyed. Council rejected a bid to have all dogs unclaimed after 72 hours from the Guelph Animal Hospital turned over to the society. In fact, by the end of 1970, all unclaimed stray dogs in the city – a total of 85 – were sold by the city, and consigned to end their lives in cages closeted in a research institution.[32] GHS no longer held the municipal dog control contract and council believed the presence of more animals at the Waterloo Avenue shelter would only magnify a noise problem it was seeking to resolve. The Society sought desperately to have animals moved from the city pound to its shelter on Waterloo Avenue to prevent pets taken from the streets of Guelph ending up in research centres.[33] City officials resisted. By early 1969, Frank Cooke was apologizing in private letters to supporters or to members of the public who complained that city officials were now responsible for the welfare of animals picked up on city streets.

One correspondent incorrectly chastised the Society for allowing only two days of life for animals picked up off the streets, not realizing that city hall now controlled the fate of strays picked up by the dogcatcher.

"As a dog owner and a dog lover, I am submitting a plea on behalf of the helpless dog, to extend the time from two to five days," she wrote Frank Cooke.

"When we were the dog control agents, we would keep a dog for an undetermined time, unless it proved by disease to be unadoptable," Cooke replied.[34] City council "turned a deaf ear to my request and Dr. (Norman) Hawkins (the poundkeeper at the Guelph Animal Hospital, agents for the city) can do as he likes with them after 72 hours." Cooke went on to describe the use of a private citizen as poundkeeper as a backward step by the city.[35]

This was not a new view on Cooke's part since he had been talking about the role of humane societies as animal control agencies for nearly a half century. "Dog catching is not really part of the work of the humane societies," he told the Brantford Riding Club on Feb. 17, 1950. Speaking as the president of OSPCA, Cooke added that "the only reason that humane societies do this work is that people have confidence that it is done more effectively and humanely than by any other organization. The prevention of cruelty is our real job, and education the most effective way of achieving that object."

---

[32] Undated clipping from the Daily Mercury (believed published in 1971) found among the Frank Cooke papers. The newspaper report, headlined 'No dogs destroyed by city reflects new canine law', noted that in 1969 the city destroyed 48 dogs and sold another 40 to research institutions.

[33] Under provincial law, the city pound was only required to keep dogs for 72 hours before destroying the animals. (Since the introduction of the Animals for Research Act on May 3, 1971, all abandoned animals in Ontario must be made available to licensed research institutions on request.) The request from the society for animals to be turned over to it from the pound was in keeping with its role as an animal welfare agency; and in conformity with a policy adopted in 1971 by Ontario Humane Society which urged societies to use a provision of the act to donate the animals to itself, and formally transfer the dogs from a city pound to a shelter. "Our thinking is, very simply, that the act specifically exempts the 'shelter' section of buildings from the requirements of the act," said OHS general manager Tom Hughes in a bulletin to societies in April, 1971. The 72-hour rule remains in effect today at municipal pounds in Ontario. However, since Guelph Humane resumed operation of the city's animal control services in 1977, it has little actual effect in Guelph. Those animals picked up as strays are turned over to the humane society as a matter of policy after the 72-hour period and are then made available for adoption. Guelph, following a formal decision of the board of directors in 1984 continues to refuse requests for animals to be used for research purposes. Most animals used in research today are bred for the purpose, eliminating a major concern among humane supporters that household pets would be forced into research.

[34] Letter to Elizabeth Shearer dated Jan. 10, 1969. GHS continues this policy today.

[35] ibid. Another letter, addressed to a Mrs. Burrows and dated June 17, 1970 referred to a December, 1969, clipping taken from the Daily Mercury which reported 27 dogs were impounded during November, 1969; eight were claimed, four were adopted, one was quarantined and "nine given for university research."

After the cancellation of the animal control contract, the society received minimal financial support from city hall, which only compounded the society's already difficult financial position. For the first time, municipal taxes were levied against the shelter property, because, Cooke was informed, the city's dog pound was no longer on the site. A four-month budget report in April, 1969, showed the society lost $1,586 on operations – an estimated annual loss of $4,637.58.[36] Council later agreed to a $300 grant.[37] The continued shelter operation on Waterloo Avenue also resulted in a continuing litany of noise complaints from neighbors, causing great stress for city council. Despite continued representations to city council, no change in policy took place.

In January, 1970, Cooke urged council to regard the Society's role as an effective adjunct to its own dog control activities and provide a $5,000 grant, the same level of support it provided in 1968. "Many inquiries are received from citizens re: Dog Control; 663 – in fact, and calls are still constant at about 45-76 monthly."[38] During 1969 GHS also removed 509 dogs and 683 cats from the streets of the city – including 173 dogs and 278 cats listed as strays that city dog control services should have been responsible for collecting and housing. On 55 occasions during the first year the city operated dog control, the society was called on remove injured animals from city streets because municipal services were not available. Cooke urged council to understand the impact of the Society's service because it reduced the potential of multiple litters and therefore larger numbers of unwanted animals on city streets, the nuisance these animals could cause ratepayers and the resulting "menace to health." The plea fell on deaf ears.

Despite Cooke's hope that council could "see the justice of financially supporting this society", only $300 was granted.[39] Meanwhile, membership in the society had collapsed due to the controversy over the location of the shelter, and the confusion generated by the on-going fundraising activities by the OSPCA which took money out of the community for provincial humane activities. In his 1971 annual report, Cooke reported only 84 members, a massive drop in support from four years earlier when the society reported a membership of 761.[40]

But it was animal welfare issues that dominated the public agenda in the late 1960s and early 1970s, forcing open debate on controversial practices of trapping and sealing, and opening the door for GHS to shift its priorities from simply shelter management to pet owner education and humane values.

Sandra Bond, speaking more directly of the work of the 1980s, said local humane societies had their hands full just trying to survive and to operate animal shelters, let alone address the many pressing concerns

---

[36] In a brief conversation with the author shortly before her death, Mrs. Nancy Cooke described how she had worked to raise money for the Society through various fundraising activities. She said that on many occasions, her husband had used his own money to keep the Society operating. The author can find no documented evidence of Frank Cooke helping the Society in that manner. However, William Hamilton, a lawyer who once acted for GHS, and knew the family socially, told the author he believed it was very possible that Mr. Cooke put some of his own money into the operation of the Society. The extent to which Frank Cooke assisted the Society financially may never be known.
[37] Letter from city clerk W. (Gord) Hall dated June 17, 1970, a response to a letter dated May 30, 1970 from Cooke which sought the grant. "Without some financial assistance from the City of Guelph, it is improbable that the society can carry on indefinitely. It will be an unfortunate situation if the society will have to cease operations through mistaken views of economy."
[38] Letter to city council dated Jan. 12, 1970 from Cooke.
[39] Ibid. It should be noted that in a follow up letter dated Jan. 30, 1970, Cooke responds to city council's request that he formally apply for a grant like other organizations. One of the points he makes is that 5,010 children in public schools in Guelph were enrolled in the Junior Humane Society. In a letter to the editor of the Daily Mercury, dated Sept. 29, 1970, Cooke noted that only $300 was provided by the city while municipal taxes were $400.
[40] AGM president's report, 1971; AGM report, 1967.

being raised by the public about animal welfare issues. This observation remains true about the activities of GHS between 1968 and 1980.

The continuing concerns about financial support illustrates the uncertainty under which an organization like GHS lived. The "traditional" humane society operations of "emphasis on good care, control and programs such as public education," were about all the society could handle during the early 1980s, said Bond.[41] While the efforts were directed toward traditional humane values, Bond noted that others were raising humane issues about hunting, fishing and trapping that had to be addressed while "we, of necessity, spend our time running an animal shelter."

"Be assured," she said, "that your board and staff are aware of the changes around them and while we can't agree with all the actions of the animal welfare organizations, neither can we condemn them all.

"Many of these groups have played a vital role in raising public awareness, opening otherwise closed doors, and generally letting in fresh air," she said.

The biggest animal welfare issue faced by Guelph and all other animal welfare agencies during this period was the announcement in 1968 that Ontario would pass legislation to force municipal pounds to turn over unclaimed animals to universities, and privately licensed firms for research.

GHS found itself in a unique position as the controversy of the animals for research law was debated in the province, it was not at that time the operator of a municipal pound, having ended its contract with the city. Therefore, it was not legally obligated to turn over animals for research. As a result, the issue, while it drew attention locally, did not have as great a public profile in Guelph as it did in other communities. Guelph had established a policy before the Second World War that it would not offer living animals for research.[42] This commitment was to be tested – and bent in 1977 – when the society sought renewal of the animal control contract. (See chapter on Animal Advocacy; the Society's representation on the University of Guelph Animal Care Commmittee.)

"We had to agree," says Bond. "City council asked us the question whether we were prepared to turn over dogs to the university, and we had to say yes. The city did not want to be held legally responsible if we, as their agent, failed to comply with the law."

Philosophically, compliance was alien to the goals of the society, a fact that was not lost on the board of directors which had to weigh the demand for live animals against the greater question of achieving a cash flow that would sustain the society and its work, and offer it an opportunity to provide direct assistance to a greater number of wildlife, dogs and cats.

However, both GHS and OVC understood the delicate political issues which surrounded the question of a demand made on an humane society for live animals. Although the institution did on a few occasions request animals for anatomy studies, GHS complied only after having an animal

---

[41] Minutes of 1987 annual meeting.
[42] Minutes of monthly meeting, April, 1936.

control officer witness euthanasia of animals that would have otherwise been destroyed in the normal course of events. Unlike city hall, GHS refused payment for the animals utilized by the institution in this manner. In 1984, the board passed a resolution refusing to turn over live animals for research, thereby formally objecting to provisions of the Animals for Research Act.

During the debate over the implementation of the Animals for Research Act many other Ontario humane societies, among them many OSPCA affiliates, found themselves at the centre of a storm of controversy. Polarized views split various groups, organizations and humane societies, more often than not condemning humane societies and the OSPCA for failing to truly represent the interests of the animals they professed to represent. This troubled OSPCA general manager Tom Hughes, who pointed out in a letter to affiliate societies in 1970: "In 1969 we were faced with a threat to the structure of the (Ontario Humane) society by (the Animals for Research) legislation introduced by the government. It seems ironic that in 1970, we should be subjected to perhaps a more insidious, and even more dangerous threat from irresponsible, fanatical, and I am quite sure, a relatively small number of our members."[43]

There was no similar philosophical debate among politicians at Guelph city hall, who viewed stray animals as just another commodity with which to make money through their sale to research institutions. According to a report in the Daily Mercury, the city sold 40 dogs picked up on city streets in 1969 to the University of Guelph, two years before the mandatory requirements of the Animals for Research Act forced city pounds to make such sales.[44] In 1970, 85 dogs were turned over by the city to the university.

The transition from the leadership of Frank Cooke to the leadership of Sandra Bond in 1973 took nearly a decade to complete. While it took longer than anyone wanted, the process was part of a long-range plan to achieve the goals of the new executive. The first few years involved raising the profile of the society while at the same time raising funds to pay for the operation of, and construction of, a new animal shelter. Later, as funds became available, a variety of humane education programs would be added as society services.

Meanwhile, GHS was working at its limit for accommodations in the Waterloo Avenue shelter and in its service delivery. "People who want to get rid of their unwanted pets, have to go on a waiting list until accommodation is available," Frank Cooke told the 1973 annual meeting.

After Sandra Bond took over the reins of the Society, it embarked on a major change in management policy that was to have a profound impact on community awareness and acceptance. The newly-formed board of directors under the Bond administration, agreed to vest operational control in the hands of its shelter manager. This was a departure from the previous policy, approved in 1968, which restricted the activities of its inspector to solely that of an animal care attendant in charge of the shelter.

---

[43] Hughes, in a form letter dated May 15, 1970, and marked personal which was sent to Frank Cooke and other selected members of the OSPCA.
[44] Undated clipping headlined 'No dogs destroyed by city reflects new canine law'.

The 1968 policy stated that "it is not necessary or desirable that the inspector go into the schools. This is the responsibility of the president or convenor of the junior humane society who is qualified both by education and experience to visit the schools." The inspector was responsible for all animals held at the shelter but "he is not the manager of the society, so (he) cannot assume any responsibility which is that of the executive of the society."[45]

The move to delegate authority was a first step toward providing a professional working environment for shelter staff. Although today this is an accepted management approach to operations of animal shelters, it was untried when implemented in Guelph two decades ago. This new direction required a new kind of person at the helm, one that had management skills and a post-secondary educational background that provided an understanding of the goals of the humane movement.

The shelter manager, in those early days of the mid-1970s, was not a position to be envied. It required dedication, commitment and long hours, as Lorna Ronald, the present manager notes:

"In early 1980, I became the manager. At the time, the manager shared responsibility for cleaning cat kennels, answering phones, animal health, speaking engagements and of course looking after the shelter. I remember well and can only look back and appreciate how long a way we have traveled in the past 10 years."

The board of directors also established a standard for the hiring of a shelter manager that called for certification as an animal health technician or veterinary health technician. If no suitable candidate was available, then the board sought a qualified AHT or VHT to be employed on staff at the shelter in another capacity. The AHT certification was first introduced into the province in the early 1970s. Centralia College of Agricultural Technology began the program, which was later adopted at four other community colleges.[46] Successful completion of the program allowed graduates to administer health care to animals, much like but not necessarily equal to the treatment a registered nurse is allowed to give a human patient.

The familiarity an AHT had with drugs administration was important for GHS. While the society required a person licensed to administer narcotics to euthanize animals, which an AHT was not allowed to do, an AHT could, however, administer non-narcotic drugs. This meant that vaccinations could be carried out at the shelter by staff rather than by taking animals to the Ontario Veterinary College, an area animal hospital, or waiting for a visit by a group of veterinary students.

Dr. Ron Downey, vice-president and veterinary adviser at the time, resolved the question of how staff could carry out euthanasia by developing a lethal dosage of non-barbiturate nicotine and caffeine-based drugs. The shelter manager can supervise administration of lethal injections, thereby removing the society's dependence on outside agencies.

---

[45] Memorandum of executive meeting held May 22, 1968. In the memo, it is also noted Frank Cooke " is acting as the general manager of the society."
[46] These are St. Lawrence College and Centralia which provide veterinary technology (three-year) programs, St. Clair and Seneca Colleges which provide a veterinary technician (two-year) program, and Sheridan and St. Lawrence Colleges which provide an animal care program.

Downey also created a vaccination program for the shelter that could be supervised and maintained by the qualified AHT. The vaccination program continues, ensuring that all animals admitted or released from the shelter receive protection from rabies, distemper and other viruses that can cause havoc in the communal kennel environment or threaten the life of an animal.

The existence of the health maintenance program became important in 1980 when Guelph was struck by an outbreak of *canine parvovirus*. The virus, which can be fatal, spreads rapidly within the confines of a kennel, and shelter staff were hard-pressed to maintain a healthy environment as animals entered and left the facility daily. Ultimately, the protocols for vaccination of animals, and the maintenance and cleaning of the shelter prevented what could have been a major epidemic.

Lorna Ronald, who was manager of the shelter when the parvo crisis struck, said the maintenance of a healthy environment is essential to ensuring that disease and illness is minimized.

"Many of the animals come into the shelter and undergo immediate traumatic stress because of being in a kennel," she said. "This stress also weakens their immune system, and that's why we vaccinate, to keep up their ability to maintain high immunity levels."

Regular cleaning of kennels and cages reduces airborne pollutants upon which virus can be spread through the facility, she added.

Sean Pennylegion, who was among the first graduates of the Centralia College program, was "exactly what the society was looking for at the time," says Downey.[47] "He had everything going for him. He had the same ideas we (the board) had about animal control, and he had a presence that commanded an appreciation for what he was saying."

Pennylegion's vision of the society's goals, were often expressed through wit and humor, which led to instant popularity among the membership, citizens of the community and among school children. But more important, Pennylegion's relationship with the local media at a time when Guelph Humane needed a strong public profile can only be described as exceptional. He was consulted on almost every story involving animals that appeared in the Daily Mercury during the 1970s, and spoke regularly, often daily, on radio CJOY about pet topics.[48]

Sean Pennylegion's legacy of work[49] continues to be felt at the shelter as many of the programs he started remain in operation today. Chief among these programs are public awareness promotions. These promotions included April being named as Adopt-A-Dog month; Adopt-A-Cat month in June, and an annual open house in December during which Santa Claus arrives to visit members, visitors, their families and children, and to leave gifts for each of the animals housed in the shelter for the holidays. In addition, the society also continues to promote Be Kind to

---

[47] Interview with author, 1992.
[48] Among the first media opportunities Pennylegion took advantage of was the Pet of the Week, a photograph of an adoptable animal published in the Daily Mercury. The weekly photo has become a regular feature in the newspaper. For the past 17 years, John MacDonald, one of the newspaper's staff photographers, has taken each of the weekly photos. MacDonald has also given generously of his time to assist the Society wherever possible. Since 1991, he's taken pet photographs for members and supporters during the annual open house held in December. Proceeds of the photo sales were turned over to GHS for the benefit of the animals.
[49] Among the first events suggested by Pennylegion was an annual open house before Christmas. The first open house in 1973 was held at the Waterloo Avenue shelter. Santa Claus made an appearance to visit the animals, the Society members and guests. Santa has reappeared each year since, leaving behind goodies for the animals and for the children in attendance.

the holidays. In addition, the society also continues to promote Be Kind to Animals Week in May, using the Saturday of the week-long promotion to hold a tag day to raise funds.

Bond, who encouraged Pennylegion's efforts, viewed them as the embodiment of the energy and commitment required for the society to work itself out of business – that is, to help bring about a universal understanding of humane values that would create no need for its services.[50] The reality is that today's humane society must continue to operate, and become innovative, in its approach to contemporary animal welfare issues.

More than $20,000 was budgeted for new cages to be purchased in 1973. However, the need for a new shelter continued to be very much evident. What held back the society was the estimated $70,000 construction cost, exclusive of the land, almost double the estimate of only six years before. Cooke maintained that society activities "were contributing to the betterment of the city and the city should be ready and willing to support the project."[51] City council did not respond other than to inquire — again, on when plans would be developed for a new shelter.[52]

Meanwhile, city police laid charges on two separate occasions under a bylaw which made the owner or person in control of a dog liable for unnecessary noise – barking.

"The first (noise) complaint came within 24 hours of the bylaw being passed," said Bond. "And a couple more were laid within the next two or three days." Bond believes city council may have acted in passing the bylaw without realizing Guelph Humane, located within a residential area, would be the first victim of any complaint.

Provincial Court Judge Henry R. Howitt, who at one time had been an honorary director of the society, eventually ruled the bylaw went beyond city hall's jurisdiction and threw the cases out of court. [53]

"What the judge said was that the neighbors, at the time they bought their properties, knew they'd be living next to an animal shelter. Because we had been there before the neighborhood, we had a non-conforming (zoning) use on the property."

The ruling opened the door to continued confrontation between the society, its neighbors and city hall. But now there was a difference. The society had every legal right to remain where it was located and continue to operate in perpetuity.

The noise bylaw charges proved a positive benefit by focusing city council and society officials on the need to finally resolve the noise problems at the Waterloo Avenue shelter. Almost immediately after the city failed to force the society to shutdown because of dog barking problems, council approached the society and renewed its offer of land on Lewis Road in the

---

[50] Comment in conversation with the author.
[51] Presidents report, 1973 annual general meeting.
[52] Letter to Milt Sather, city treasurer, from Cooke dated Feb. 3, 1973. Cooke complained about a $500 grant in 1972 which hardly covered the cost of municipal taxes. The accumulated deficit had reached $40,701 and the society was seeking a decision on a new location for the shelter. The $25,000 project of 1968 had now grown into an estimated $70,000 project, not including the cost of the land.
[53] Daily Mercury, March 23, 1974. Cost of legal services to fight the first charge in 1973 was $800, almost as much as the $806 deficit the society reported for the year. However, Peter Anderson, the young lawyer who represented the Society on the noise bylaw charges never billed GHS. Since then, Anderson has provided continued, and much appreciated, legal assistance for the Society.

The Guelph Humane Society Shelter constructed in 1974 and expanded in 1990.
Photo: Bob Rutter

city's northwest industrial park. This property, which Frank Cooke had rejected before because of its location, was again rejected by the society. However, it was – as Sandra Bond describes – love at first sight when offered the present site on lands next to the water pollution control plant.

"It had everything we could think of," she said. " It was next to the sewage treatment plant, the only neighbors close enough to complain. Behind it was the Dolime quarry which was far enough away, and with all the noise from its own operations, would never hear the noise from the animals. There was an awful lot of grassy area to walk the dogs."[54]

Within four months of the unnecessary noise bylaw being thrown out of court, the city approved a building permit for Len Ariss Construction to construct the present shelter at the water pollution control plant on Wellington Street.[55] Designed to hold 70 animals, construction costs were estimated at $68,000 with an additional $18,000 required for interior furnishings.[56] It was officially opened Dec. 8, 1974. City council allowed the society to lease the present shelter property for $1 a year.

The new shelter came on stream at a time when the society was in transition and facing a funding crisis. But it was needed for a variety of reasons, not the least of which was that the crowded Waterloo Avenue shelter was creating a poor image that offset the positive efforts volunteers and the executive were making to promote the organization within the community.

The $86,000 project to build the new shelter was partly paid for from accumulated capital investments which covered only about half the cost. The remaining funds were raised through a mortgage and paid off by the efforts of the Society's project committee and through donations from members of the community.

---

[54] Interview with Sandra Bond, 1992.
[55] Actually, the shelter was just moved down Waterloo Avenue. Wellington Street became the address when the Silvercreek Parkway and Waterloo Avenue intersection was realigned.
[56] Daily Mercury, Aug. 2, 1974.

In what must be the biggest understatement of year, Society shelter manager Sean Pennylegion was quoted by The Daily Mercury shortly after the move to the new shelter as saying the Waterloo Avenue location "was, well, rather noisy." And the newspaper noted in an editorial[57] that the entire Waterloo Avenue neighborhood breathed a collective sigh of relief. They were joined, however, by the board of directors and supporters of GHS who had fought for so long to achieve a goal of constructing a modern facility that would be an asset to Guelph. Since the shelter was moved to its new site, there have been no complaints about its operation.

[57] Daily Mercury, Nov. 15, 1974.

"I will not kill or hurt any living creature needlessly, nor destroy any beautiful thing, but will strive to save and comfort all gentle life, and guard all natural beauty upon the earth."
John Ruskin

A question of jurisdiction

The Ontario Society for the Prevention of Cruelty to Animals (OSPCA) was created in 1919 by the legislature as the official agency in the province to administer animal protection laws. One of the society's mandates was to foster the formation of local societies throughout the province.

By the late 1960s, however, there was a feeling among smaller independent affiliated societies of the OSPCA that their interests were not being taken seriously. The thought that the OSPCA was working more for itself than its affiliates was particularly galling for Frank Cooke, president of Guelph Humane, who considered himself "the savior of the Ontario society" for having prevented its insolvency during the 1940s when he had served as president. In addition, he did not believe the provincial agency could deliver the kind of services necessary, nor could address immediate local needs the way a local society like Guelph could.[1]

Guelph had contributed significantly to the development of the OSPCA before ending its affiliation in 1970. Two Guelph members had served as presidents of OSPCA: Frank Cooke, from 1943-53, and Frank Baker in 1942.[2]

Although the catalyst that spawned the move to end the relationship began with a visit to the Guelph animal shelter by OSPCA general manager Tom Hughes in 1968, the story really seems to begin in 1955 when Hughes was general manager of the British Columbia SPCA. Hughes and then OSPCA president E. M. Saunders lobbied strongly for the creation of a national SPCA organization whose membership would be limited solely to provincial agencies. Cooke, who was to become a founding director of the Canadian Federation of Humane Societies (CFHS) in 1956, opposed such a move. Had the Hughes-Saunders recommendation been adopted, the CFHS would only have been able to register membership from four provinces.[3] Small independent humane societies like Guelph feared that a national organization dominated by large groups like OSPCA would overwhelm them, and their voices would not be heard.

"No doubt you have seen the letter emanating from the Ontario SPCA," Cooke said in a letter to Ernie Jones, president of the Ottawa Hu-

---

[1] Letter to local affiliate societies from Cooke dated June 18, 1969. The Guelph society was a charter affiliate member, and continued to support the provincial agency until 1970. What caused it to sever the relationship was a series of events that caused Frank Cooke to believe the OSPCA had embarked on a deliberate policy of trying to take over small, independent humane societies.
[2] Letter to Mrs. Kathleen Young, of Toronto, dated April 25, 1970. Cooke went on to note that he was president of the OSPCA during "very difficult" years "and (I) have now lived to regret it."
[3] A Brief History of the Canadian Federation of Humane Societies by K.G. Switzer, p. 4. The four societies that would have qualified for membership were: B.C. SPCA, Canadian SPCA (Montreal), Ontario SPCA and Nova Scotia SPCA. Tom Hughes voting for the B.C. organization supported the formation of the CFHS but called for the name to be a "national SPCA." Ontario, which abstained, did not join the federation until 1962 and Toronto Humane joined in 1967.

A Century of Caring

mane Society, in early 1962. "I thought it in very poor taste jubilating that B.C. and Ontario now control the national society, and will set out to make the CFHS a federation of provincial societies. The president urges the other societies instead of joining the CFHS to let the provincial society act for them! I suppose this was cooked up in the hotel bedroom by Ontario and B.C. while we were attending to the real business of the convention."[4]

One of the requirements for membership in the CFHS demanded by OSPCA when it joined in 1961 was the right of 44 votes at the board table. B.C. sought 28 votes. There were at the time only 33 CFHS members, each casting a single vote and it was clear to the federation that OSPCA wanted to dominate the organization and have complete control. Ultimately, B.C. received one vote, the balance of the 28 votes it sought were already held by affiliate members of the federation. But when CFHS offered a compromise of 10 votes, OSPCA rejected the offer.[5] At the 1962 CFHS annual meeting held at Guelph's Parkwood Motel, the OSPCA tried unsuccessfully to seat 44 delegates. After being rebuffed, OSPCA and representatives from British Columbia and Manitoba, then tried a week later to have the annual meeting declared invalid.

Hughes left B.C. to join the OSPCA in 1962, and immediately raised the ire of affiliate societies. He demanded that inspectors employed by each society report solely to him, demanded audited financial statements from each of the independent societies through requests made directly to the inspector, and revoked identification and warrant cards for many of those already employed as inspectors.

These actions created animosity among some affiliate officials, including Guelph's Frank Cooke. A jurisdictional confrontation resulted, and local societies which were required to raise funds in their communities to pay the salaries of the inspectors protested.[6] On one occasion, Hughes telephoned the manager of the Essex County Humane Society and told the manager he was working under his (Hughes') jurisdiction and his employment had nothing to do with the (Essex) president or her board.[7]

The appointment of inspectors had always been under the control of local authorities but those societies then required approvals from OSPCA. The OSPCA Act gave the inspector the authority to investigate cruelty complaints and to lay charges under the Criminal Code, and gave the provincial society authority to control aspects of the inspector's activities. In other words, Hughes was acting within the scope of the act, however, he was making demands that had never been made before. More importantly, this was viewed by small societies like Guelph as an intrusion on local autonomy without benefit of a policy change by the OSPCA board of directors. As a result, OSPCA's activities became increasingly suspect among the smaller independent societies.

---

[4] Letter to Ernie Jones dated Jan. 22, 1962; original found in the files of the Canadian Federation of Humane Societies.
[5] Letter dated Feb. 5, 1963, to Peter Armour, president OSPCA from Sen. F.A. McGrand, president, CFHS. "It became obvious from your refusal to come in with a ceiling vote of 10 votes that the Ontario society was unwilling to join unless it had by virtue of 44 votes, to control and dominate the federation," McGrand wrote.
[6] Letter dated Dec. 21, 1963, to Peter Armour, president, OSPCA, from E. W. Jones, president, Ottawa Humane Society. Jones states in part Ottawa HS is "not adverse to accepting suggestions from Ontario SPCA as long as suggestions are forwarded through proper channels, i.e. president or managing director." He further adds: "It is the considered opinion of the directors that the Ontario SPCA under its new general manager has moved too quickly without sufficient consultations with affiliated societies and without due regard to their local autonomy." Jones called for restoration of "harmonious" relations between OSPCA and all local societies.
[7] Unsigned letter dated Dec. 7, 1962, on letterhead of Handbridge Electric Ltd. from Kathleen Handbridge, president of the Essex County Humane Society to Frank Cooke.

"The OSPCA might have been excused in its early months of their general manager's actions on the grounds its officers might not have been aware of his methods of operating," wrote Ken Switzer, managing director of the Ottawa Humane Society.[8] A particular concern for Switzer was a proposal to amend OSPCA bylaws to overcome objections to Hughes's actions by "requiring affiliated societies to apply for membership each year after promising to co-operate fully with the OSPCA."[9] It was clear, he added, that "it seems a pity so much time and effort has to be wasted in needless controversy."

Responding to the call for the cancellation of warrant cards and return of inspector badges, requiring the recertification of affiliate society inspectors, Cooke called for an amendment to the OSPCA Act to "restrict membership of the board or executive committee to accredited delegates from humane societies only."

The purpose, Cooke wrote officials at four other societies, "is clear – the humane societies must obtain control of the OSPCA which is being run to the detriment of humane societies by non delegates" who did not represent the affiliate interests.[10] That was only one of the avenues explored by Frank Cooke. In December, 1962, he suggested to Ken Switzer that "we have to get nominations in for a new board that will kick out this little clique that is disturbing us all."[11]

Additionally, the proposals made by Hughes were only a first step because about one year later he made suggestions for changes to the OSPCA Act of 1955 which would remove local autonomy from affiliated societies.[12]

By 1968, six years after Hughes took over the helm of OSPCA, he had taken the OSPCA budget from $36,000 to $360,000 and equipped inspectors and wardens with police style uniforms. Trucks sported an official legal-style logo, and he was opening animal shelters around the province at the rate of two a year. But after he suggested salaries for his inspectors equivalent to that of an Ontario Provincial Police corporal, George Hulme, general manager of the Toronto Humane Society said he was empire-building. Hughes rejected the charge.[13]

The sense that OSPCA was undermining the status and role of independent societies was still very much an issue in 1968. "The humane societies in the province created Ontario SPCA and helped keep it alive," said Cooke. "Now it is so strong that humane societies are gobbled up and become branches. We have created a juggernaught which may destroy us."[14]

---

[8] Letter to Frank Cooke from Ken Switzer, managing director, Ottawa Humane, dated Jan. 26, 1963.
[9] ibid.
[10] Copy of letters sent to George Hulme, Toronto Humane Society; Mrs. D. E. MacKay, Lincoln County Humane Society; Judge J. de N. Kennedy, Peterborough Humane Society; and K. G. Switzer, Ottawa Humane Society; dated Feb. 19, 1963.
[11] Letter dated Dec. 10, 1962, to Switzer from Cooke. In the letter, Cooke notes: "I hear that Toronto is not supplying him (Hughes) with financial statements and that they will not recognize his authority." Guelph provided an operating statement for 1961, "nothing more," Cooke wrote.
[12] Letter to Kathleen Handbridge, president Essex County Humane Society, from Walter H. Prince, solicitor for the society, dated Jan. 17, 1964. "It is quite clear that if Mr. Hughes is successful in obtaining the proposals put forward by his brief (dated Oct. 25, 1963), it would be a giant step forward towards attaining monopoly by the Ontario SPCA. In supporting the amendments proposed by Mr. Hughes, the Essex County Humane Society would lose most of its local autonomy, and in time, might very well become little more than a branch of the Toronto operation." Prince suggested political action through Essex County members of the legislature to fight the proposed amendments. But he also suggested the ECHS take the initiative: "It is the writer's further belief that to preserve this local autonomy, consideration should be given to take the appointment of inspectors out of the jurisdiction of the Ontario society and place it in the hands of the attorney-general's department."
[13] Globe Magazine, July 27, 1968. The rank of OPP corporal no longer exists. All corporals were promoted sergeant during a reorganization of the force in the mid-1980s. The effect of Hughes' desire to increase salaries would have been to double the amount of money being spent on inspection and enforcement of cruelty laws, the funds for which would have had to be provided by the local societies that employed the inspectors.
[14] Copy of letter to Mrs. Alexis Ignatieff, president of the Ottawa Humane Society, dated April 4, 1968. Cooke was complaining about the slate of officers proposed for a meeting of the OSPCA. In his letter, Cooke called for action by Toronto and Ottawa societies which, he claimed, were strong enough to take on the provincial

Hughes visited the Guelph shelter unannounced in June, 1968, with an OSPCA inspector, and a reporter and a photographer from the Globe and Mail.

The Globe Magazine reported that "within a half hour, (Hughes) had criticized the condition of the shelter, seized a cat, condemned a row of cages and removed the (OSPCA affiliation) certificate from the wall." Hughes gave the Society one month to be cleaned up. The Guelph Humane Society, which had never taken direction from Hughes in the past, nor had allowed him to address its board of directors, refused. As a result, the certificate was never returned, although Guelph continued to be affiliated with OSPCA until its annual meeting of 1970 ratified a resolution taken by the board of directors to end the 50-year relationship.[15]

The split with OSPCA was based, not only on the 1968 visit, but also on the part played by OSPCA in a controversy that led to the GHS relinquishing its animal control contract with the city, fundraising activities of the OSPCA within the City of Guelph, and because Hughes refused a request in 1969 to issue a warrant card a for a newly-hired Guelph inspector. Cooke, pressing Hughes to defend his decision to refuse the warrant card, was told simply that according to the OSPCA Act he (Hughes) did not have to say anything to defend his action.[16]

Although Hughes stated in a letter to Frank Cooke[17] the 1968 shelter visit was not tied to a newspaper story on the GHS, photographs of the society dominated a feature story on Hughes published in the Globe Magazine. In the letter, Hughes justifies his actions because he claimed to have received "a number of complaints from different sources concerning facilities in the shelter and some practices followed by the Guelph Humane Society."

Cooke was on holiday in England at the time of the visit. The GHS board felt the actions of Hughes were unwarranted, particularly because it came on a morning when the normal regime at the shelter had been interrupted by an employee who went home about 9 a.m. after reporting for work, and by a flat tire on the society's ambulance which had to be repaired so that a truck load of trash could be off-loaded at the dump before being returned to normal society duties.

Hughes, who walked into the shelter about 11 a.m., rejected all explanations about why shelter staff had not completed cleaning animal cages, or why the truck had not been cleaned prior to some animals being loaded for delivery to the Ontario Veterinary College where they were to be destroyed. Hughes was particularly upset about the animals in the ambulance, especially after learning the animals were in transit to OVC where they could be used in research.

Ed Latta, the employee who was confronted by Hughes, was following instructions left him by Cooke when he went on vacation. In an unsigned

---

organization. The letter was apparently in reply to one received from Mrs. Ignatieff. In it, Cooke states: "I acknowledge receipt of your report re: the Ontario Humane. It is disconcerting, to say the least, to find such lack of co-operation."

[15] A resolution moved by director Mr. Young and seconded by Mr. Stephens on March 18, 1970, approved the deletion of the words " in affiliation with the Ontario Humane Society" from the bylaws of the Guelph society. There is, however, some confusion about the affiliation severance because Guelph paid its 1970 affiliation fees to OSPCA. The fees were $25, and not the $100 that Tom Hughes had requested, according to correspondence written by Frank Cooke to E.E. Harris, of Galt, on Feb. 25, 1971.

[16] A series of correspondence in April and May 1969 between Hughes, James Andrews, then-secretary of the society, and Cooke.

[17] Letter dated July 11, 1968 from Hughes to Frank Cooke.

note in Cooke's handwriting dated June 2, Cooke told Latta he was in charge of the shelter because of the unexpected resignation of Insp. James Cosgrove. And, Cooke said, Latta had the right to issue orders. If anyone was insubordinate, "you have power to replace them." But more importantly, Latta was instructed: "Unadoptable dogs and cats are to be taken to the college promptly for humane destruction. Only such animals that can be adopted should be kept beyond the 72 hours."[18]

Cooke, who had maintained a particularly good relationship with the Ontario Veterinary College, was upset that Hughes also attacked the integrity of the College by questioning whether GHS animals were actually destroyed, or kept alive for research. A better idea, he said, would be to destroy the animals at the shelter rather than by taking them to OVC.[19] Hughes appeared more conciliatory about his comments on OVC when he wrote Cooke two weeks after the visit. Hughes said he "was not suggesting for one minute that animals supplied by the Guelph Humane Society to the college are being used for research, but obviously the necessary assurance can't be given by the officer."[20]

Eventually, in 1972, Hughes' suggestion was implemented. Applauding the veterinary college's "close co-operation and practical assistance", Frank Cooke told the 1973 annual meeting "twice weekly, two or more veterinarians visit the shelter and examine the animals there and treat them when necessary. They also put to sleep those who are too old or diseased."[21] This program was supervised by Dr. Ron Downey who was to later serve as president of the GHS.

This question of OSPCA fundraising would become a thorny one in Guelph, especially after Guelph severed its affiliation. But it was a minor issue compared to the more pressing concerns GHS had about the need to replace its shelter on Waterloo Avenue, which had been a cause of bitter feelings among neighbors and members of city council.

It was the issue of replacement of the shelter which exacerbated the tension that already existed between Frank Cooke and the OSPCA. After Hughes visited the shelter in 1968, and removed the affiliation certificate, he commented on the need to replace the shelter with a newer more modern facility. Those comments would have a profound impact on the GHS, and lead to further confrontation over jurisdiction and authority. In his letter to Cooke, Hughes said: "The solution to the problem is to obtain a more adequate contract with the City of Guelph and then build a modern animal shelter."[22] A new shelter was achieved six years later but only after repeated stalling from city council, compounded by the intervention of Hughes and the OSPCA in telling the city it could provide a better ani-

---

[18] Unsigned note dated June 2, 1968, found in the Cooke papers. This note was based on a resolution approved at the society executive at its May 22, 1968, meeting which changed the job description of its inspector. The inspector was now to confine his work to within the city limits of Guelph. Since the Guelph inspector also provided services as a regional inspector in Wellington County for OSPCA, the resolution effectively restricted the operations of the OSPCA enforcement operation. The action was taken by Guelph to better control the movements and workload of Insp. James Cosgrove.
[19] Copy of letter dated Oct. 21, 1968, to Premier John Robarts protesting the use of provincial grant money to the OSPCA to "harass an institution with so fine a reputation as the veterinary college, which is staffed by capable and kindly disposed doctors." Robarts, who replied Jan. 27, 1969, did little to intervene. "We are aware of the difficulties . . . (which) are receiving the consideration of the government," Robarts wrote. "I am sorry that you are subject to this harassment and am happy to have your expression of opinion."
[20] Letter to Frank Cooke dated July 11, 1968. Hughes reminded Cooke in the letter: "I am sure you will appreciate that it is against the bylaws of the Ontario Humane Society for any animal to be supplied alive to any research institute or laboratory." He then gave assurances that "if carcasses are required by the college, then we have no objection to these being released."
[21] President's report, 1973 annual meeting.
[22] Letter to Cooke, July 11, 1968.

mal control service — and operate a humane society in competition with the GHS.[23]

There is no reply in the Cooke papers from the OSPCA to his concerns that the OSPCA had deliberately tried to discredit the Guelph society by removing the affiliation certificate in 1968.[24] Cooke chose to seek redress by going to the Canadian Federation of Humane Societies, lobbying the support of individuals and long-time humane society supporters, writing to the minister of agriculture who was responsible for enforcing the OSPCA Act, the minister of justice and the attorney general, and by writing George Drew, chancellor of the University of Guelph.

"While the indefensible treatment of your society by Tom Hughes is strictly outside the jurisdiction of the federation, I feel that since your society is a member of the federation, the incident should be properly reported in the minutes of the (annual general meeting) followed by some expression of disapproval," said Judge John de N. Kennedy, president of the Federation.[25]

But 12 days later, the good judge replied that he had failed. "No one seemed forewarned that the Guelph society intended to make a formal complaint of the treatment it received from Tom Hughes," Kennedy wrote.[26] If the ground work had been laid, Kennedy believed the complaint could have been heard by the federation. CFHS, instead, passed a resolution calling the dispute between Guelph and the Ontario society an internal matter, and all references were stricken from the record of the federation's annual general meeting.

Eventually, Drew's secretary acknowledged the letter in which Cooke urged Drew to seek support of the province which "could with wisdom, discretion and justice, reduce or cancel the grant on which (OSPCA) thrives. The continual harassment of the (Ontario Veterinary) College and the Guelph and other humane societies is sufficient cause for such action." There is no record of Drew taking the advice, nor is there any suggestion the OSPCA felt threatened by the call for action.[27]

In 1971, Cooke's concern about apparent OSPCA efforts to takeover small societies got support from an unlikely source: E. E. Harris, of Galt, a member of the South Waterloo Humane Society and a director of the OSPCA for seven years, resigned from the OSPCA board because he had lost "faith in the present policies of the (OSPCA) board (and) its abilities to cope with the ever recurring problems of management."

---

[23] Letter to Garth Macdonald, of Oakville, from Frank Cooke, dated Oct. 24, 1968, reported the OSPCA had contacted city council sometime in the intervening three months and offered to provide animal control services. Noting the Ontario society was critical of the GHS, OSPCA suggested it could provide a "virile humane society" because it operated eight animal shelters and five more were under development. Cooke scoffed at the "professional" approach the OSPCA talked about because it suggested the Guelph, which was the first community in the country to have a municipal animal control contract operated by a humane society, had been providing the service for 20 years.

[24] The author visited the OSPCA offices on several occasions to review material. However, the best that could be offered was a scrap book of newspaper clippings dating back to the late 1960s. OSPCA officials did not know that Frank Cooke had been president of the provincial agency for 10 years.

[25] Letter to Frank Cooke from J. de N. Kennedy dated Nov. 13, 1968.

[26] Letter dated Nov. 25, 1968.

[27] Despite the publicity and the acrimony that resulted from Tom Hughes's June, 1968, visit to the Guelph shelter, there is no mention of the incident in the report of the 1969 OSPCA annual meeting.

In a letter of explanation to all affiliated societies and branches of Ontario Humane Society, Harris noted that "certain incidents that had occurred since the latter part of 1969[28] (which) had caused me to have doubts about . . . various matters."[29] Harris went on to note that "it is the admitted desire of the general manager that all affiliated societies should eventually become branches of the provincial body, and he is being encouraged in this by some board members."

This was an important comment from Cooke's view because it appeared to vindicate his belief about OSPCA and its goals.

"We are an autonomous society and do not need the Ontario society, except that he (Hughes) has legislation passed that he only approves an inspector, and without this legal approval our legal status is challenged," Cooke said in reply to Harris.[30]

The disagreements between Cooke and Hughes also frustrated fundraising activities for both societies between 1969-71 which was a very slow period for financial contributions to the Guelph society. The publicity which would result from the confusion and confrontation also caused some concern for the Guelph branch of the Bank of Nova Scotia, which held a special account for OSPCA donations generated in the area. In an undated 1969 monthly report, Cooke notes that the manager of the bank informed him that OSPCA was about to start another fundraising campaign in Guelph.

"Mr. Brown (the manager) had apparently met with some criticism and bad publicity over the campaign last year," Cooke noted. "He wanted to know if there would be any publicity in the paper. I said that we might have to inform the public that we had no part or benefit as a result of the campaign." In a letter to the bank dated Dec. 17, 1969, addressed to J. Black, (sic) manager, Cooke called the literature "dishonest in its intent to deceive people into believing that a branch of the Ontario Society exists in Guelph. Surely, it is not in the best interests of the bank to allow itself to be a party to this deception. For donors may well think they are making a donation to the Guelph society when the money will actually be going to Toronto."

In a letter to OSPCA president Gordon Trent, Cooke protested about the flood of appeals by the Ontario Humane Society delivered to every city household: "The Guelph society has ceased to be affiliated with the Ontario Humane Society" yet during this period mass mailings by OSPCA to Guelph sought donations for:

- The Guelph branch of Ontario Humane Society – which didn't exist;
- The Burlington branch of Ontario Humane Society ;
- The Grand Valley branch of Ontario Humane Society;

---

[28] Harris referred to disagreements about Hughes's management role in dealings with the Niagara Frontier society, an affiliate agency, and the Brantford society, a branch of OSPCA.
[29] Letter dated Feb. 17, 1971, to all affiliates and branch societies.
[30] Letter dated Feb. 25, 1971 to E.E. Harris

- The Ontario Humane Society[31] which used a post box at a local bank to solicit these donations.

Tom Hughes justified mass mail fundraising campaigns in a letter to the editor of The Daily Mercury. "Recent publicity in your newspaper may have tended to confuse the public . . ." he wrote in what was certainly an understatement.[32] The mail fundraising campaign protested by the "Humane Society in Guelph and Wellington County (sic)"[33] was part of a province-wide effort each year "except in those parts of the province where the local society contributes towards the cost of an inspector."

Hughes made the point of stressing that Guelph now did not have an inspector, failing to tell readers of the newspaper that he – and he alone – had authority under the OSPCA Act to appoint a replacement inspector in Guelph; or that he had refused Guelph's request to appoint an inspector for the city.

"I'm quite sure," Hughes admonished readers, "that the people of Guelph are interested in protecting all animals from cruelty, not just the fortunate few who happen to live in the City of Guelph."

Money raised in Wellington County is spent in Wellington County – "and more besides", Hughes said, contradicting a comment in the same letter in which he said the OSPCA was dependent on charity for its work and "it will be necessary for us to appeal to people who live in the denser urban areas such as Guelph" to protect millions of animals living in the rural areas.

Eventually, the mass mail fundraising campaigns became less an issue as a change in GHS leadership, and a higher community profile for the society increased its membership and afforded new fundraising opportunities.

Six years after Cooke had tried unsuccessfully to return the OSPCA to its original mandate as an umbrella group for its member societies, he tried again at the OSPCA annual meeting in July, 1969.[34]

The letter proposed a slate of seven delegates for nomination to the OSPCA board from independent societies. Cooke signed the letter – on Guelph Humane letterhead – on behalf of the Guelph society, as a past president of OSPCA, and for the Niagara Frontier Humane Society, Ottawa Humane Society, Oakville Humane Society and the Toronto Humane Society. Guelph, stung by the 1968 confrontations with OSPCA,

---

[31] Guelph was not alone in being targeted for fundraising by Ontario Humane. In an undated letter to the president and directors of OSPCA, Alexis Ignatieff, president of the Ottawa Humane Society criticized similar actions by OSPCA in Eastern Ontario. "We wish to place on record that the Ontario Society has deliberately conducted a campaign for funds in Ottawa knowing that the Ottawa Humane Society was then engaged, and still is, in trying to raise funds for its new shelter. By no stretch of the imagination can the Ontario Humane Society justify sending 50,000 letters to Ottawa, 25,000 to Toronto and none to certain other cities," she wrote. OSPCA "must not confuse the general public who support us . . . for the more the Ottawa Humane Society can do the more effort the Ontario Humane can put into other areas."

[32] Letter to editor, Daily Mercury, Jan. 4, 1969

[33] Guelph had officially dissociated its activities from Wellington County in 1966 by formally changing its name, and by approving a 1968 memo preventing the society's inspector from working outside city limits. These were facts that Hughes should have known since Guelph was still an active OSPCA affiliate at this time.

[34] Letter to local affiliate societies from Cooke dated June 18, 1969. In the letter, Cooke calls for a return to the "function of the OSPCA . . . which is stated in its bylaws – fostering the formation of local societies throughout the province." Instead, the provincial agency's "principle activity . . . consists of the establishment of branch committees which are not encouraged to become independent."

and several other affiliate societies were clearly upset. The affiliates were particularly concerned that OSPCA's 16-member board of directors only had four delegates from the independent societies, a clear violation of OSPCA bylaws which called for a minimum of eight affiliate delegates to be appointed or elected to the provincial board.

Guelph and the affiliates sought to renew the OSPCA's mandate by seeking policy changes which included:

- giving a strong leadership and positive encouragement to local societies that were OSPCA members;

- encouraging branch committees operated by Ontario Humane to become independent where practical;

- establishing a uniformly high standard of animal protection and enforcement across the province.[35]

The effort apparently failed because one month later, Tom Hughes issued a statement to local affiliates outlining amendments being sought by the Ontario Humane Society to the OSPCA Act that would centralize control of enforcement of all animal welfare legislation with the provincial agency.

Using the Royal Society for the Prevention of Cruelty to Animals as a model, Hughes, among other changes, called for "appointment, supervision and employment of inspectors only by the Ontario Humane Society; (and) . . . that any society operating in Ontario (as a humane society) must make a percentage of their revenue available to Ontario Humane to meet the expense of inspectors."[36] It was a move designed to consolidate power and authority under the control of the provincial agency; a far cry from the noble efforts taken by Cooke and the affiliate societies one month earlier who sought to decentalize the operations of the OSPCA.

Hughes justified the proposed changes, saying they would strengthen the enforcement of animal welfare laws and ensure that the Ontario Humane Society was funded adequately to carry out its duties.

"The situation revolves around funds," Hughes admitted.[37] "A local society raises funds from a centre of population. An appeal is made by the local society for "humane work". Unfortunately, the definition of humane work and the way that money should be spent is at the discretion of the directors of the society at that time the directors change from time to time and the priorities change accordingly.

"Ontario Humane Society is faced with an impossible task. We cannot raise sufficient funds by traditional methods to make possible the appointment of an adequate force of inspectors throughout the province."

---

[35] ibid.
[36] Letter to presidents of affiliate societies and presidents of OSPCA branches dated Aug. 18, 1969, from Tom Hughes, general manager, OSPCA. These proposed changes were then sent to the attorney-general for action. Affiliate and independent societies were never asked to fund the operation of OSPCA directly, as outlined by Hughes.
[37] ibid.

To those who opposed the mandatory funding of OSPCA from independent societies, Hughes said that method was "far more satisfactory and efficient than the present one. Satisfactory, that is for the welfare of the animals."

Frank Cooke continued to oppose many policy actions taken by OSPCA until he retired in 1973. Since 1970, GHS has been one of a handful of local humane societies across the province that has no affiliation with OSPCA. Relations between the two societies are cordial today, but there is no desire on the part of Guelph to rejoin the provincial society.

"No one can hazard a guess as to how many millions of humans have died in the past from milk from diseased cows. Disease brought on in most cases from contamination from accumulations of filth. It was the humane societies (that) exposed the vile conditions prevalent before the appointment of sanitary inspectors, and they are still bringing to court offenders who do not maintain their stables and barns in a sanitary manner."
Frank H. Cooke,
president, Ontario Society
for the Prevention of Cruelty to Animals
in an address to the Brantford Riding Club
Feb. 17, 1950

Demand escalates need for larger facility

Sandra Bond and Dr. Ron Downey worked hard to improve the profile of the GHS in the eyes of the public, and strived to gain both memberships and donor dollars immediately after taking over the leadership of the society in 1973.

It was at this time that two important events happened, almost coincidentally: The society hired Sean Pennylegion as manager, an energetic young man fresh from college who promoted the society and its work endlessly; and Pennylegion met Joanna Watkin, manager of Willow West Mall.

Willow West Mall, located at Silvercreek and Willow Roads, was at the time the only major shopping mall outside the downtown core. It was popular because of its location in the burgeoning growth area of west Guelph.

Watkin opened the doors of the mall to allow Guelph Humane to set up a booth to promote information about humane education and to solicit memberships.

"Joanna's patience and understanding was pivotal to us," said Bond. After taking over the operation of the society, "it was vitally important to get out to the community, and Joanna helped us do it.

"The membership list per se, could not be established (in 1973). Donors who were listed were asked to renew memberships, but we needed many more members."

Joanna Watkin
president 1979-81 and 1983-84
Photo: Joanna Watkin

That first public display was a traumatic experience, Bond recalls. "Our display was a (card) table and chair and a newsletter – two typewritten pages stapled together saying we are here and we care, and some information on our situation. But the important thing was, we were there, in the open, talking to people."

Watkin was surprised, more likely stunned, by the amateur display. She called Pennylegion to confirm that this was the Guelph Humane Society's display, and then came immediately to the Society's assistance.

"She accepted (the display) and supplied us with some table cloths and a lot of understanding," said Bond. In two days at the mall, 45 new members were enrolled, many of whom said they "didn't know we were there and that they would be there for us if we needed them."

Watkin was to eventually become a member, a volunteer, vice-president and later president (for five years) of the Guelph Humane Society. "Through the years, I was happy to do something for animals who have given me so much; love, comfort and companionship," she said.[1]

The leadership Watkin gave is best illustrated by her attempts to get wildlife artist Robert Bateman to give a public lecture in Guelph, and to donate signed prints of his work, all in aid of the society.

"I recall driving through an Ontario snowstorm to interview him; the visit was marvelous compensation for the heart-thudding journey," Watkin said, who now lives in Peterborough, England.[2]

Members of the 1992 Junior Humane Club with some of the shelter animals. From left: Jonathan Uyede, Kelly Woltman (front), Sandra Woltman, Susan Dunkley, Jacqueline Gillard (co-ordinator), Dana Brown, Lindsay Moore and Kristy Finnigan.   Photo by Bob Rutter

---
[1] Comment to author, January, 1992.
[2] Comment to author, January, 1992. Joanna writes that she lives on the "western edge of the wide-open, sky-filled Fens. Her husband is working on land reclamation and mining, employed by a large environmental and engineering company. I continue to write and photograph, do publicity for a music festival and am getting more and more involved with crafts, particularly textiles." She lives with four felines. Allegra, "snow white and Wagnerian in build if not in voice"; (Dizzy) Gillespie, "a human in furry pajamas; pretty quiet Esmeralda and her youngest, Dau Bach, talkative (mouth actually), feather-weight and very affectionate." were all adopted in Canada from the Guelph animal shelter. They survived four months in quarantine to join the Watkins at their home in England.

Longtime volunteer and member Margaret Puzey with Diamond, a shelter mascot for 14 years. After her death, she provided the Society with funds to establish the humane values program. Peg, as she was affectionately known, is seen wearing a fake fur jacket, a concession she made to style and an example of her concern for animals.
Photo: John MacDonald

Once the shelter was opened in 1974, the Society spent much of the next six years working to pay off its $86,000 cost. This placed an enormous workload for the staff, board and volunteers. By 1980, GHS was operating programs to promote pet ownership responsibility and education of awareness of health, animal control and animal breeding issues. Services provided by the society included free veterinary examinations for animals adopted from the shelter,[3] cat identification tagging, spay/neutering of adoptable animals at the shelter and visits by shelter mascots to senior citizen homes, schools and prisons.

When Bond and Ron Downey took over leadership of the Society, the immediate goal was to get the operation back on a solid financial footing. Recapturing the animal control contract became a central goal.

"It was an important move for the society," said Ron Downey. "We needed the cash flow to help pay for the mortgage and to keep the shelter going."[4]

The Society was very vulnerable to financial difficulties during those days of the mid-1970s, Bond said. Stable funding through a monthly cheque from city hall was a goal that had to be achieved. But it would take about four years for the new Society executive to reach agreement with the city.[5]

---
[3] There were 23 area veterinarians taking part in the free examination program., the 1992 annual meeting was told.
[4] Conversation with Dr. Ron Downey, 1992.
[5] Conversation with Sandra Bond, 1992.

A Century of Caring

That's where the present treasurer, Janet Daly entered the picture. "There were good people before her but she came on at a particularly difficult time," said Bond. "The new shelter had just opened and we had a lot of work to do to clear up what today looks like minor debts . . . of about $14,000 but it was a lot of money in those days and that had to be addressed."

Bond said she "duped" Daly into taking on the job by promising "it would be not more than four or five hours a week. I knew it would be far more than that."

Daly set to the task and made some unpopular management and budget austerity moves that angered staff from time to time. It is not simply the long-term commitment to the volunteer position that has made Daly a well-respected member of the executive, it has been her demonstrated leadership, Bond said. "We were two times blessed by having her."

Often during the early years of her tenure, Daly would be in the shelter every day, spending several hours, keeping the books straight and looking to improve methods of revenue collection.

"At that time, we didn't know where our money was going to come from," said Bond. "We haven't missed a payroll, and that's incredible for an organization that is not government funded," said Bond.

The greatest contribution Daly made, however, was looking ahead and investing where possible whatever cash surplus existed at the end of the year. Bond calls this a natural action by a frugal, Scots woman dedicated to the humane cause. The proceeds of these capital investments today help the Society fund some educational programs, and is also intended to offset shortfalls in fundraising.[6]

Janet Daly,
treasurer since 1976
Photo: Bob Rutter

While this was happening, Guelph had two close calls with exotic snakes that got lost in high rise apartment buildings. GHS assisted city officials in formulating a bylaw banning the ownership of exotic animals within city limits.

The Society's intervention in the snakes affair may also have broken the ice with city council. Shortly afterward, city hall made it known to the executive that if it could prepare an animal control contract proposal it

---

[6] This investment strategy will pay dividends in 1993 as the recession of 1989-92 has created difficulties in fundraising, forcing the Society to use some of the accumulated capital to meet operational expenses for the first time.

had good chance of being considered seriously for the 1977 budget year, said Bond.

Negotiations for the resumption of the contract were cordial, open and without the acrimony that was evident during the contract negotiations of the final days of 1968. In the end, a new contract was achieved; one that contained new elements for animal control that would have been unheard of only a decade previous.

"Our goal from the start had been to get the 'dog control' contract and turn it into an animal control contract," said Bond. "Not once; not in any correspondence or in discussions did we use the term dog control.

"And we did something that no one else did; we hired people with an animal health background who knew how to care for the animals, especially those hit on the road. This gave us a better chance of getting animals to OVC alive."

The city recognized that animal control went beyond dogs and ultimately included the collection and emergency medical treatment of stray cats. This was a remarkable concession on the part of the city because it marked a recognition of the true humanitarian role of the Society.[7]

City council "made it very clear to us that part of our workload would include the pick up of dead animals, and that included large numbers of wildlife," Bond said. "We are dealing with death and disposal here; and it was our feeling that if we're asked to care for them dead, we should be concerned about them when they're alive. And, that the municipality should also be concerned."

When Bond appeared before the finance committee to make the pitch for more support than just dog control, she said two of the most influential members, Ald. Ken Hammill and Mayor Norm Jary, offered solid support for the proposal. But it may have been for selfish reasons: "I know from discussions with aldermen that they were sick and tired of receiving after hours calls because there was no one else (at city hall) to receive them.

"The city's service only operated from 8 a.m. to 4 p.m., and that didn't work

Betty Stone
director, chair of capital fundraising for the shelter expansion
Photo: Betty Stone

---

[7] It also marked a major shift in council's fiscal position on providing the service. Under the Dog Licensing and Livestock and Poultry Protection Act, the city could only collect taxes – dog license fees – on dogs. The provision of the service was primarily to reimburse farmers from the dog license fees for livestock kills attributed to dogs running at large. Although people scoff at the thought that a community like Guelph has problems with dogs attacking livestock, the city does have several operating farms within its limits. The city must also appoint a livestock evaluator to oversee any investigations into livestock kills. The authority contained in the livestock protection act were transferred to the Ontario Municipal Act in 1990.

A Century of Caring

because often kids come home from school at that time, and sometimes the dog would get out. We were here for the animals and their needs and that doesn't necessarily happen between eight and four and only on week days."

The executive also made it clear to city hall that animal control was a municipal responsibility that must be funded adequately to carry out the service. GHS was not about to get itself back into a position of subsidizing the municipality because its own humanitarian mandate appeared to overlap that of the city.

"It gives the Society a certain prestige to operate the animal control contract, and it shows we are here on behalf of the city of Guelph and we're not just a group of well-meaning people out to educate the world." About the same time as the negotiations for the animal control contract were developing, the shelter embarked on a new source of fundraising: profits from the sale of pet food and accessories sold from the shelter.

City hall was less than enthusiastic about the Society selling goods from the shelter in competition with local merchants. It was felt that since the shelter was located on municipal land, there was an unfair advantage. City hall didn't seem to understand that sales were generally geared to the Society's membership and only those members of the public who visited. Nor were the sales generally advertised within the community in such a way as to compete with local merchants.

However, when a proposal to renovate the shelter for better use of storage space, and a larger retail area, was made in 1978, the project was placed on hold indefinitely after discussions with city staff revealed it

The 1992 project committee, whose work is part of the lifeblood of the Society, meeting in the board room of the shelter. From left seated: Eva Darling, Bruce Jones and Dorothy Mathieu. Standing from left: Diane Gilbertson, Susan Blair, Marj Leib, Joyce Runge, Helen DeBaan, Edna Jones, Barb Farr, Jan Brett (chair), and Jacqueline Gillard.
Photo: Bob Rutter

could become a sensitive political issue.[8] The sales of pet food and accessories continued, however, and these sales represent a significant source of revenue for the society.[9]

In 1979, the second year into the animal control agreement with the city, the Society found it was facing greatly increased calls for service. A growing city provided greater numbers of animals which had to be housed in the shelter. For example, in 1980, the society answered 4,239 calls, or an average of 11.6 per day, which was a 50 per cent increase from 1979. By 1989, the figure had risen to 5,809 calls, or an average of 16.1 calls per day, and the Society was responsible for patrolling a geographic area about one-third larger than 10 years before.[10]

The executive immediately realized that the new animal shelter, which was to provide adequate service for 20 years was rapidly becoming too small. Plans for expansion were discussed, but greater priorities existed in maintaining the animal control contract and offering programs that met the goals of the Society.

The 1970s could be called a learning period for a new executive, treading warily into uncharted waters, seeking to make giant waves with little more than a paddle. But much was accomplished, although it was often at the expense of gaining experience on-the-job, and by treading water financially. The decade of the 1980s, however, turned into a period of satisfaction and reward as the Society worked quietly to achieve its goals. There was no controversy, no confrontation with city hall, and no conflict over long-range goals.

GHS's development of defined humane education programs, and it's slow integration of animal care services as it could afford to make improvements was seen by many humane societies in Canada and the United States as progressive and sound.[11]

By the end of the 1970s, GHS provided services to:

- shelter stray cats until adopted or reclaimed;

- reunite animals with lost owners;

- offer a humane education program for public and separate schools on a voluntary basis;[12]

- rent harmless traps for relocating nuisance wildlife and stray cats;

- provide law enforcement agencies with specialized information on cruelty or distress complaints involving animals;

- operate a food terminal for members of the society and the general public visiting the shelter.

---

[8] Author's notes from discussions with city engineer Ray Funnell and Ald. Peter Brazolot, 1978.
[9] In 1991, revenues from food and oat litter sales accounted for $19,285. Animal accessory sales accounted for a further $16,462. Fees from adoptions in 1991 generated $44,961.
[10] Data from the shelter manager's animal control report, 1980 and 1990 respectively.
[11] Conversation with Sandra Bond, 1992.
[12] Operated on a the basis of an invitation from a teacher, this program would be approved by the boards of education by the mid-1980s, and all classrooms in elementary schools throughout Wellington County would participate.

Dr. Ron Downey, who helped establish the free veterinary examination of adopted shelter animals by local animal hospitals, also assisted in creating the program in 1978 for the spay/neutering of shelter animals by third year students of the Ontario Veterinary College.[13] The first Guelph area veterinary to join the free examination program was the team of Dr. David and Dr. Paulette Jolley.[14]

"I worked closely with him in getting this program off the ground," said Lorna Ronald, the present shelter manager.

"We organized OVC students to come into the shelter weekly and examine the animals before surgery. From September, to December of 1979, over 70 animals were sterilized, increasing their chances of being adopted and minimizing the shelter animals from contributing to pet over-population."

The spay/neuter program has prevented the premature death of hundreds of animals that were made more adoptable through the surgery, while also promoting the society's goal of reduced pet over-population. There are two elements to the spay-neuter program: that which is provided through assistance from the Ontario Veterinary College; and the subsidy of spay-neutering surgical costs for members of the public.[15]

GHS promotes kindness to animals through its junior humane club, and employs shelter animals to bring joy to those shut-in by illness, disability or those incarceration. The success of these programs, combined with the promotion of the Society's spay/neutering policies resulted in Guelph being awarded the first annual Canadian Federation of Humane Societies Model Shelter Award for 1986.[16]

The Junior Humane Club was rekindled in 1982 by Kathy Elliot, then shelter manager, and Sandra Solomon. Operating today as a voluntary membership rather than by subscription as it was in schools many years before, the club meets at the shelter, usually in Saturdays or Sundays and discusses various animal and pet-related subjects. This promotes not only a sense of compassion and humane values among the membership but has also created many lasting friendships among the young people it serves. Since 1983, the club has entered a float in the annual Guelph Santa Claus parade.

A spay/neuter subsidy program was introduced in 1987, funded in part by a $1,000 cheque from Canadian Federation of Humane Societies (CFHS) in recognition of the model shelter award. The program allows families or individuals which can't afford the cost of spay or neutering to receive a subsidy of as much as 30 per cent of the cost of the surgical procedure from funds raised by the society. Pet over-population is a serious urban issue, one which GHS has attempted to view on a global scale

---

[13] The establishment of the two programs was not without controversy. Dr. Downey was brought before the ethics committee of the Ontario Veterinary Association (now the College of Veterinarians of Ontario) by a local private practice veterinarian. The association eventually rejected charges that he was preventing private practice veterinarians from offering services to spay neuter and to examine adopted shelter animals. Dr. James Archibald, dean of OVC, defended Downey's spay/neuter program because it provided a practical surgical experience for veterinary students.

[14] Dr. Paulette Jolley is today a director of the society and its chief veterinary adviser. Dr. Downey is now assistant dean of OVC, and the faculty member responsible for promoting the college's Centre for the Study of Animal Welfare. He was given the first appointed in 1992 to the Ontario Veterinary College's Chair of Animal Welfare. Sponsored by a $500,000 endowment from the late Col. K.L. Campbell, Downey's role is to explore ways to encourage and support alternative investigative methods that reduce, refine and replace the use of animals in research, including research that is aimed at improving the quality of life of animals in general. Campbell, a noted horse breeder and showman, and his wife Mona, were among the earliest contributors to the University of Guelph's Pet Trust program.

[15] In 1987, for example, the society gave out 30 certificates to assist pet owners in having their pets spayed or neutered. Pet owners are free to take their pets to any veterinary for the surgery. By 1992, 50 certificates (the maximum available) were being issued during March of each year, Spay/Neuter month.

[16] In the category of communities with a population under 100,000.

while making a significant local contribution. A national strategy for reducing unwanted and unloved animals in Canada is being assisted by the CFHS. GHS contributes 50 cents for each animal surrendered and $1 for each animal adopted to the Canadian Federation of Humane Societies Animal Surplus Fund. This money is earmarked for helping develop programs that will reduce the numbers of animals.

"The (CFHS) award is tangible recognition of the society's work to educate people in all aspects of responsible pet ownership," John D'Alton, a reporter with The Daily Mercury wrote when the CFHS award was announced.[17]

One of the factors that gave Guelph the CFHS shelter management award were statistics on the number of reclaimed animals. In 1986, the Society had a reclaim rate of 18 per cent by owners who retrieved lost cats, more than four times the national average of about four per cent. The reclaim rate for dogs was about 60 per cent, up about 10 per cent from the national average.[18]

The figures reported for 1986 are an indication of the success of the Society's cat tagging program, and a requirement that all dogs leaving the shelter be licensed with a City of Guelph tag.

"We tag cats, every cat that comes in," Bond said. "Any cat that comes in as a stray and goes home always leaves with a collar and the Guelph Humane Society identification tag. It's mandatory. You don't leave here without some form of identification.

"It's not the law, but we've never had any problem with that policy because people see the benefit to tagging that cat. If the stray had had a GHS tag, it might have been home a long time before the owner eventually found it at the shelter."

The cat tag program began in 1974 after Sean Pennylegion visited relatives in British Columbia and discovered a similar program. The cat tags are kept on file until the animal is reported dead – even today a records remain from the very first year of operation. Since its inception, cats found as strays in communities as far away as Montreal and Prince Albert, Saskatchewan, have been returned to owners because the animals were wearing a Guelph Humane identification tag.

"Many people don't realize the work we are doing," said Lorna Ronald, shelter manager, following the announcement of the award at a convention held in Hamilton. "I'm not saying we don't make mistakes . . . yet I challenge anyone to come down to the shelter and leave with criticism."[19]

An elementary school teacher hired by the Society visits every school classroom in Wellington County as part of the humane values program. Taking along a shelter mascot, usually a well-trained dog, the teacher spends time with schoolchildren teaching them about respect for animals, pet ownership, kindness for living things and humane values. This program, a leader in the field of humane education across Canada, is dedi-

---

[17] Clipping from Daily Mercury, 1987.
[18] Shelter manager's annual report, 1986, delivered at the 1987 annual meeting.
[19] ibid.

cated to the memory of Margaret (Peg) Puzey, a long-time supporter and energetic volunteer, who left a $20,000 bequest to the society to help fund the initiative in 1987.[20]

During the first school year, 1987-88, more than 200 kindergarten to Grade 6 classes were visited at Guelph public schools. In 1988, the Roman Catholic separate school board approved the program, pushing the number of classrooms to 350. In late 1990, the program was extended into all of Wellington County which expands classroom participation in the program to 640.

In late 1991, GHS analyzed the statistics from the past five years and reported "some positive and interesting results which can be attributed to humane education":[21]

- the number of dogs and cars housed in the shelter decreased by nine per cent;

- the claim rate for stray animals increased in 1987 and remained constant;

- the adoption rate for dogs and cats increased in 1987 and again in 1990;

- the euthanasia rate decreased by 10 per cent;

- and, probably the most significant statistic, animals struck by cars dropped 30 per cent in 1990.

"I'm very proud to be a part of such a stable humane society," said Ronald, who was first hired as an animal control officer in 1977, later became shelter manager. Ronald retired briefly, but continued to be involved in the society by serving on the board of directors and chairing committees including junior humane and humane education. She returned as manager in March, 1986. Shortly after her return to management, Ronald became a visiting inspector for the Canadian Council on Animal Care, and joined the Association of Animal Shelter Administrators of Ontario where she had held several executive positions including treasurer. In 1991, she was elected a director of the Canadian Association of Animal Shelter Administrators, and became vice-president of the Central Canada Region in 1992.

"We are in a new era of advancement and I feel enthusiastic in a new and different way. We are increasing our awareness and conversing with other shelters as well as the Canadian Federation of Humane Societies. People are beginning to notice us as a dedicated shelter, and also our competence as administrators.

"Our service to the community is commendable and is mainly accredited to a strong, supportive board (of directors)."[22]

---

[20] The program's impact has been great, not only among educators but also with humane activists. Information about how the program was started and implemented has been sought by several humane societies across Canada and the United States. Susan Porter, a long-time member of the Society and an elementary school teacher, helped develop the program and its curriculum. After it was in operation for a few years, she took a leave of absence from full-time teaching to become the Society's teacher of the humane values program. She now lives in western Canada
[21] Shelter manager's report, 1991.
[22] Shelter manager's report, 1987 annual meeting.

Ronald's comments reflected an awareness of the role of the society built on her work as an animal control warden, shelter manager and a member of the board of directors.

"Up until the time I came to GHS, I didn't have a positive outlook on humane societies," Ronald said. "On my arrival in September, 1977, there were strict policies in place, a vaccination program for shelter animals and a cat tagging program. It was very impressive for the era; and so were the cleaning and disinfecting programs."[23]

As the Society was making inroads into achieving its educational goals, work with the animals was involving greater and greater numbers, placing stress on the 'new' shelter. The need for a new shelter was reaching a critical point, and in 1987 the board of directors approved an expansion of work and kennel areas of about 2,000 square feet, bringing the facility to a total of about 5,000 square feet.

The new expansion would provide the GHS with isolation areas for both dogs and cats, a board room that can double as a workroom and kitchen, a larger number of dog runs, and increased kennel areas for strays and those held in the municipal pound.

"It was our ambition to be able to get the animals out together (for exercise) rather than the rotational business we had been enduring," said Bond.

After much negotiation with the city – although very much less confrontational than during the negotiations during the 1960s – the new addition was approved and the board of directors accepted a tender valued at $145,946.[24] Gorgi Construction completed the project in 1990 and the expanded shelter was officially opened by Mayor John Counsell, a long-time member and supporter of the Society.

This project also marked a first for the Society that was little noticed by the media, or for that matter by many members: it was the first time GHS would embark on a capital campaign without seeking municipal funding assistance.

"So often groups just go to the public first but we plan to go once we have raised our part internally," said Betty Stone, a director and chair of the capital fundraising committee.[25]

Stone, whose volunteer work in Guelph is almost as legendary as that of Maude Pentelow's was for GHS, called on the board of directors to spearhead the capital campaign by each making donations before the general membership was called on to assist.[26] It was a challenge they accepted and the capital campaign benefited through its leadership by example. Stone set out to raise the nearly $200,000 required to both build and equip the new facility. By September, 1989, Stone was informing donors that $115,000 had been raised, a very large amount of money in such

---

[23] Conversation with author, 1992.
[24] Minutes of tender opening March 28, 1989.
[25] Clipping from Daily Mercury, 1989. Confirmed in conversations between Sandra Bond and the author, 1992.
[26] An elementary schoolteacher at King George public school, Stone is best known for organizing and establishing the annual Terry Fox Run in Guelph. Among the groups and agencies she has at various times served – sometimes concurrently – are the board of Family and Children's Services, the Wellington District Health Council and city council.

a short time, nearly all from donations from the public, the board of directors and more than 700 Society members. [27]

Two significant fundraising events, both of which were large-scale and both of which raised large sums of money for the Society, were held in 1989. The first, a dinner at which author and cartoonist Ben Wicks was the guest speaker, raised about $6,500 drew more than 400 members, guests and supporters.[28] The second, an auction of donated goods and services by local businesses and individuals – well over 150 items, some including framed original and lithograph art work – was held at the Guelph Holiday Inn and raised nearly $4,500.

"We realized that the real impact of our fundraising was alerting the people to our needs," said Bond. "We don't own the Society (although it is an incorporated entity). Everything we do is for the animals and the community.

"But when it came to asking for the funds, we realized that the City of Guelph is asked to give and give and give. So we didn't ask, and this project was done without any government assistance whatsoever."

By the time the new shelter expansion was opened in 1990, almost all the money required for the project had been raised. Dog runs, which had been a $20,000 cost of the original expansion, were completed in 1991 when all the funds became available.

The shelter expansion was required because the work of animal control, and humane shelter services were increasing in response to Guelph's growth, both geographically and by population. The 1989 animal control statistics show 5,809 calls were logged by Guelph Humane, 4,268 of which were direct requests from the public. Animal wardens issued 287 bylaw infraction tickets, impounded 5452 dogs, picked up 701 dead animals from city streets, sold 491 dog tags for the city, rented 68 humane traps, picked up 525 stray cats, 1,000 birds and wildlife, treated 461 injured animals, responded to 109 animal in distress calls and traveled 41,093 kilometres in the society's ambulance to provide the service.[29]

The society reported to city engineer Ray Funnell in 1989 that after hours calls for service had increased in three years from 995 to 1,211.[30]

To this date, the contract with the city allows the Society to operate only during daylight hours for capturing dogs running at large; capturing and confining stray animals; removal of dead animals from city streets; the rescue of injured animals; and to respond to complaints of animals in distress or those being abused. Emergency responses are provided after hours for injured animals; confined stray animals; animals in distress or abused; and "any catastrophies" reported.[31]

---

[27] Letter to donors prepared by Betty Stone dated: 89 09 04; and a clipping from The Daily Mercury.
[28] Clipping from Daily Mercury, 1989.
[29] Surprisingly, there were only six barking complaints and two complaints about violations of the city's stoop and scoop bylaw.
[30] Letter to Ray Funnell from Janet Daly, society treasurer outlining the society's proposed $128,175 1989 animal control budget. The number of calls reported in 1986 was 995; and 1,042 in 1987. The society also collected $5,607.25 for the city in fines, fees, board, administration and skunk removals. In part, because of the impending celebrations of the Society's centennial but more so to draw attention to the its concerns about pet over-population and the increasing numbers of animals being handled by the animal control officers, GHS in co-operation with Maclean Hunter Cable Television produced a video presentation entitled *Reining Cats and Dogs* in 1992. The video is expected to be rebroadcast during the centennial celebrations in 1993.
[31] Services Information sheet dated February, 1988.

The society's animal control officers were sworn in as bylaw enforcement officers in 1977 when the animal control contract was returned to the society. This authority gave the animal control wardens authority to enforce the dogs running at large, and the licensing provisions of the bylaw.

"The image of the dog catcher with a net is over and a new era of the caring, professional animal control officer was beginning when I came to the society," said Ronald. "Animal control was in its growing stage and we were learning the ropes by trial and error. There never was a dull moment.

"I learned quickly that not all people were kind to animals or people," Ronald said. "As an animal control officer, I did everything from climbing up into attics after raccoons to chasing bats in businesses downtown; to high-tailing it back to the van to avoid being eaten alive by Zorro, a mammoth black dog that delighted in eating mailmen."

But being an animal warden also had its good points, especially when there was a mutual affection develop between officer and animal.

"On a day in 1979, I picked up a massive St. Bernard on Paisley Road," Ronald said. "It took me over an hour to earn her trust and get her into the van. Lucy became our mascot and was loved dearly by all. She died in 1986 at the age of 12 years. She became well known as part of the pet visitation program and for her visits to classrooms throughout the city."

Lorna Ronald, shelter manager
Photo: The Daily Mercury

Cruelty investigations are carried out by police with assistance from the Society's officers and staff where necessary. At other times, Society staff assist the OSPCA and Ontario Provincial Police with area investigations. Most notable among cruelty investigations in the past 20 years was a raid on a Puslinch Township home where several dogs were seized during an investigation of a dog-fighting ring. The raid resulted in the conviction of an area man in 1976 for training dogs for fighting. More recent cruelty investigations have included the arrest of a man responsible for throwing a puppy to its death from a high rise apartment.

"You used the word destruction. For years, even we at the society were hiding behind the word euthanasia but we have to learn to say the word kill. We are killing animals, and we're doing that on behalf of a negligent public. We kill far too many animals because people have made so many of these animals unwanted."

*Sandra Bond,
interview with author, 1992*

Animal advocacy

The Canadian Council on Animal Care (CCAC) awarded its first Award of Excellence in 1992 to the University of Guelph for its operation of research facilities at the Equine Research Centre, the Ponsonby Research Centre and the Arkell Bull and Ram Test Centre. The award, which honors the university's animal care staff and the institution's Animal Care Committee, was made in recognition of their combined effort to offer facilities that provide exemplary care standards. It also recognizes the provision of an environment that respects the animals and the quality of life they live within those facilities.

However, the award also indirectly spotlights the Guelph Humane Society's efforts during the past century to act as a community conscience for animals housed at the institution. In the early years of the past century, faculty at the Ontario Agricultural and Veterinary Colleges provided advice, information and on occasion medical assistance in the day-to-day operation of the humane society. These informal contacts helped keep the issues of animal welfare in the city, and on campus, in focus.

The informal relationship between GHS and the Ontario Veterinary and Agricultural Colleges dates back to its very beginning. However, it was more formally acknowledged in 1927 when Dr. W. R. J. Fowler became the first president of the society after it adopted a role dedicated solely to animal welfare.

Fowler was the first of three Ontario Veterinary College faculty members to serve as president of the GHS. He was a veterinarian with an international reputation, and a Guelph resident who contributed much of his life toward the betterment of the community by serving on many boards and commissions. His greatest contribution, however, may have been the start of a tradition of assistance for Guelph Humane by OVC faculty, staff and students.[1]

During his tenure as president, Fowler tried unsuccessfully to have city council install special equipment to destroy unwanted animals.[2] Thereafter, much of the assistance provided by OVC included the emer-

---

[1] The other two are Dr. Lionel Stevenson and Dr. Ron Downey.
[2] Minutes of GHS, 1928.

gency treatment of animals taken in by the Society or the destruction of unwanted animals.[3]

The relationship evolved over the years to become an important element in GHS's ability to provide a high level of service to the community, especially during the Great Depression and immediately following the Second World War. It was a special relationship that drew the envy of many other humane societies across the province. Thank you letters, copies of which were located in the Frank Cooke papers, attest to the generous donation of time, service and medicines by faculty and students at the college.

It was not, however, a one way street. In return for this assistance, the society offered many young veterinary students a chance to experience off-campus practical study by allowing examinations of shelter animals; the treatment of ailments and medical emergencies; the spay/neutering of shelter animals by third year students; and, until 1974, the destruction of many unadoptable animals held at the shelter.

The Ontario Veterinary College continues to provide a 24-hour emergency service which is often used by the society for road-injured animals. Birds and wildlife, which now make up a notable portion of the society's work are also treated by the college's veterinary teaching hospital or at the university's wild bird clinic.

Today, the society has a recognized presence on campus through the appointment of Sandra Bond to the university's animal care committee. When Bond joined the committee in 1984, 22 years after the committee was established, it marked the first time in Canada that a community advocate for animal welfare was appointed to an academic research institution watchdog committee. The university's decision to appoint Bond was made voluntarily about one year before the council on animal care mandated research institutions to appoint a community representative to animal care committees.[4]

The council on animal care was formed in 1968, partly as a response to growing public concern about the use of animals in research, and also to establish standards for use of animals by the scientific community. Increasingly at this time, there appeared to be a siege mentality among parts of the scientific community. It was not difficult to understand why. During the 1960s, the international humane movement was riding on a crest of rising public support. The Humane Slaughter of Animals Act was passed by the House of Commons in 1959 after active lobbying by the Canadian Federation of Humane Societies (one of the very reasons the federation was formed) and many local societies, including Guelph. This had been a long battle, dating back to the turn of the century. Campaigns to save seals, to save whales and to find more humane trapping methods were also prominent and high profile issues. GHS supported many of these activities through its membership in the national federation, and

---

[3] This was acknowledged in a letter to Dr. J. H. Reed of the Ontario Veterinary College on July 5, 1972. In the letter, Frank Cooke notes the society's " thanks for your own contribution, and also that of your colleagues for the work you are doing at the society's shelter. Your medical attention is of the greatest value to the animals in our care and adds reputation to the society. We also appreciate your good offices in the very necessary and painless and instant euthanasia for those animals which are unwanted and unadoptable." According to a note found in the Cooke papers, the society "put to sleep" 447 of 1,129 dogs brought to the society in 1971. The note indicates 480 cats were also destroyed.

[4] Conversation with Sandra Bond, 1992.

by keeping a local watch on research being conducted at the university on seals and humane trapping.

Appointment of a community representative is the university's committee is an important accomplishment for the society. It is also a lot of work. Each research protocol must be reviewed by the committee for acceptance, rejection or modification. All protocols which require the use of animals must explain how the animals are to be used, and provide details of any invasive surgical procedures. In 1989, the committee reviewed 600 protocols; by 1991 the number had jumped to 1,072.

"I view this as important work and find it time consuming but often rewarding," says Bond. "This gives me first hand knowledge of the use of animals in teaching and research at the university. A look into any laboratory is preferable to ignorance."[5]

Initially, Bond was seen as an outspoken animal advocate, but also as the "enemy," someone to be viewed with apprehension and concern by some members of the scientific community, said Dr. Denna Benn, director of animal care services at the University of Guelph. This view slowly ebbed, and today Bond is recognized as an open-minded community resource person, bringing with it a respect for the advocacy she represents.

"When I first sat in a room in which everyone in that room was or is an animal researcher, it was very difficult," she recalls. "I didn't have a science background and the first batch of protocols that came before me was nothing more than gobbledygook. We were constantly dealing with terminology that I was always having to look up. To this day, there are some that I have to lookup, but not as much."[6]

"Sandra is an ideas person," Benn said. "She's the kind of person we throw ideas off of; who answers questions and addresses issues with forthright honesty."

Bond's contribution to the committee is more than just addressing the questions raised by research protocols; it is also responding with sensitivity to the general needs of the 100,000 animals at the university, about 80 per cent of which are poultry or fish.

While the commitment is great, Bond believes it is better for a community representative on the animal care committee to be "someone who brings their thoughts and worries home with them rather than someone that goes home and dismisses it as inconsequential or unimportant."

During the first two years of participation on the animal care committee, Bond admits she was unduly quiet. Part of this was related to learning the background of the scientific community, becoming acquainted with the position, understanding the research being undertaken at the university, and respecting the confidentiality that is an accepted part of the research community.

However, it was a constant fight to remain objective, holding back her views that no animal should be used in research. "Do we have the right to

---

[5] President's report. Minutes of 1989 annual meeting.
[6] Much of the comments attributed to Sandra Bond were made to the author during conversations in 1992.

use animals? It is something I have never wholly answered," she says. "I don't know if we do have that right."

But the university's animal care committee does give the community "the opportunity to voice our concerns and, generally speaking, I come away and I have been convinced those concerns were unwarranted, or changes were made that one can accept in these procedures."

As a member of the institution's animal care committee, Bond also has the right to visit unannounced any research facility on campus, says Benn. Each week the committee makes visits at several of more than 30 sites on and off campus where animals are being used for research.

As a director of the Canadian Federation of Humane Societies since 1986, and an executive member since 1987, Sandra Bond also provides the university with an insight into issues of animal welfare that have surfaced at the federal government level.

The committee was expanded in 1990 to include two community advocates, a concession to concerns by Bond that the amount of work required was far greater than a single representative could handle.

In addition to Sandra Bond's role on the animal care committee, Lorna Ronald, the society's shelter manager, has also inspected university facilities as part of the CCAC's triennial inspection and assessment team. Her role as an inspector for the CCAC is not limited solely to the University of Guelph. She has also been part of teams that have visited the University of Waterloo and many private laboratories throughout the Waterloo-Wellington area.

The efforts by Bond to raise consciousness and awareness about animal welfare issues coincided with a move by the University of Guelph to address the question of the ethics of using living animals in research. Courses were developed to discuss the morality of using animals for research, and to instill in researchers an awareness that animals are living beings with sensitivities that must be respected.

The debate was not new; it has been part of the public agenda for decades. However, it came to prominence again in Ontario in 1968 when Queen's Park released a discussion paper that proposed what was eventually to become a statute governing the use of animals in research.

Compliance with the requirements of the law were rarely enforced, and there are less than half a dozen occasions when the society was forced to provide animals to licensed research facilities. Acceptance of this policy ended officially in 1984 when the GHS board of directors approved a resolution refusing to turn live animals over to research institutions, notwithstanding the dictates of the Animals for Research Act.

"We sent a copy of the motion to the Ontario Veterinary College (in 1984) informing them of our policy, and we trusted that they would not put us into non-compliance (of the Animals for Research Act) and they have not done that," Bond said. "We have been treated very fairly by the University of Guelph and they have been very sensitive to our position. The word shelter, if you look it up in the dictionary, really means sanctuary, and we felt that it was not fair to an animal to send them on to another place for all types of (research) procedures."

Guelph was not the first humane society to refuse to comply with the law, but it was also not the last. The motion to end compliance marked a rite of passage for the society, a point where animal control activities ceased to be its raison d'tre.

"Although we understand there is a need for valid research," says Lorna Ronald, "we feel strongly that animals that were lost pets are not suitable."[7]

Researchers agree, but for different and more selfish reasons, says Benn. Today's research often requires animals that have a defined background; the uncertainty of a pet's health can often negatively influence scientific data, necessitating a repetition of the experiment.

"If animals are necessary, they should be bred and raised in research facilities because of the emotional trauma that can be felt by a (household) pet being brought into that kind of situation," said Ronald.

More and more, that's what is happening, Benn said. Animals are bred within institutions for the precise purpose of various types of research. The advent of genetic and biotechnical advances means that animals can be born with conditions that fit directly into research priorities.

While this is taking place, the university is aware also that the debate over the use of animals will continue. Efforts continue to find ways to reduce the numbers of animals being used.

"We're well on the road to getting more exact animal models (through tissue culture and other alternatives). I don't know what that will mean in numbers but in the old days, it was 50 or 60 and we're now down to five or six."

"We have gone from using 360 rabbits to something like three or four a course," says Benn. This reduction in numbers has been a slow evolution, something she described as "a creeping mass" that over-took the teaching profession somewhat by surprise during the 1980s. Many of the changes instituted in teaching during the past decade – audio-visual presentations, tissue culture experiments and biological engineering for specific purpose" have been suggested by students, many of whom care passionately for the animals they share laboratory space with.

"What's happening," says Benn, "is that people are more and more making decisions on the side of the animals."

All these changes come at a time when animal research funding at the university has increased dramatically, from $32 million in 1986 to $60 million in 1992.[8]

"Even with the kind of increase in money, we are still decreasing the numbers of animals being used. We are winning the battle to reduce numbers," she said.

---

[7] In 1986, the Ottawa Humane Society, which provides a small number of animals each year to the University of Ottawa, explained its policy to its members this way: "Why does the society provide animals for research? Because we live in a world where there are many surplus cats and dogs which have to be destroyed because no one wants them; because we live in a world of much illness in both humans and animals; because, for certain illnesses such as heart disease and cancer, there is as yet no substitute for research using animals; and because the animals that the society provides for research suffer no pain and contribute to human well-being." Only animals brought in under animal control operations and unclaimed – never animals left at the shelter by concerned owners or citizens – are turned over for research. Pressure from membership and from other animal welfare agencies contributed to the OHS changing its policy about three years ago.

[8] Conversation with Dr. Denna Benn, 1992.

"The greatest need today, in my opinion, is not money but workers, supporters and sympathizers. The payment of a membership fee – be it one dollar or one hundred dollars – doesn't necessarily enlarge our field of support."
**Frank Cooke,
president of the Guelph Humane Society,
speaking before the
Canadian Federation of Humane Societies
when it met in Guelph in 1962**

And a final word

Volunteers are the lifeblood of the GHS. From the many who join the organization in spirit, there is often little more than a handful of people who are committed to working diligently to keep the Society a viable community service. The contribution they make can't be measured, nor can words adequately express the gratitude they deserve.

Fundraising is usually the prime focus of the volunteers, although others take part in administrative tasks like serving on the shelter management committee. GHS sponsors annual garage and book sales, and promotes the sale of various products including pet accessories, cheeses, garden seeds and beauty care products developed without testing on animals.

It takes all kinds of people to help GHS operate. But most important, it means that those who make donations, or provide their time have an interest in animals.

"Some people are in a position to donate time, others are in a position to donate money and don't have the time," said John Runge, president 1990-92. "I think you need both kinds of members to make it very successful."

Runge, who has been involved in many community organizations, said, "the people with the Humane Society seem more dedicated and involved than in many other groups."

One of the greatest moments for the volunteers was in 1980. The project committee realized it had raised enough money to pay off the $4,000 remaining on the mortgage for the

John Runge, president 1991-92
Photo: John Runge

A Century of Caring 83

construction of the animal shelter. This money was raised through diligent effort, and by a willing community that has supported the activities and events sponsored by the Society.

Although the most prominent fundraising activities are those that are visible, the project committee's smaller efforts reap great rewards for the Society. For example, through the energy of a handful of individuals, GHS has placed and maintains donation coin boxes in 56 stores, restaurants and shops throughout the city.

Several supermarkets also provide support through cash rebates or merchandise awards based on cash register tapes collected from members and supporters. These 'small' efforts account for as much as $25,000 in funds collected each year.[1]

Seventeen years ago, when Edna Jones started the coin box fundraising program by placing boxes in two stores, Foodland supermarket and Royal City Cleaners, she viewed it as "a little extra that could pay for the hydro bill at the shelter."

"When we collect today, it takes a lot of time to roll the coins," Jones said. "There's at least $100 in pennies. But it's the pennies that add up to the dollars."

Edna's husband, Bruce, looks after the grocery tape fundraising program. He catalogues and audits all the cash register tapes that are collected by members and supporters. The Jones' are one of several husband and wife teams who assist the Society, making their contributions a truly family commitment.

In the late 1980s, the Society also began to ask its supporters to make donations through a unique commercial program sponsored by Zellers, a large retail department store. Zellers, which has two stores in Guelph, opened special accounts for each patron into which points based on purchases were held for redemption of goods at a later date.

An account in the name of GHS was taken out in 'Club Z' and the details communicated to the membership. The success was overwhelming. By 1989, the Society had received 460,000 points.[2] But most importantly, the points were turned into the free purchase of goods required by the Society. These included:

- a video cassette recorder for use by the humane values program;
- office furniture and equipment;
- and cleaning and maintenance supplies, estimated to have saved the Society $300 during 1990-91.[3]

GHS is one of a few volunteer organizations which does not have an annual volunteer appreciation night. That is by design, although it doesn't mean the efforts of the volunteers go unappreciated, said Sandra Bond. What it means is that all this effort goes directly to the dogs – and cats,

---

[1] During the first half of 1992, GHS received about $3,500 from supermarket cash register tapes, and another $4,000 in loose change deposited in the Society collection boxes.
[2] Shelter manager's report, 1989.
[3] Shelter manager's report, 1991.

so to speak. For most of the members and volunteers who support the Society, that's thanks enough, and it has its own inner rewards.

"All the money given by members of the Society, and all the money raised from the community is spent on the animals and we try to keep the administration costs to a bare minimum," said Bond. "That's been our underlying philosophy of the Society, and to spend the money on ourselves is to take that money away from the animals.

"By having volunteers going out into the community and doing fundraising, you are touching on people that are not members, don't want to be members but are happy to contribute on a one-time or occasional basis. That's how tag days and bazaars have become successful, and continue to be held."

Volunteers also give the executive a sense of the need and of the quality of the service GHS provides. Contact within the community, and also among staff members, allows the Society to accept, often implement and promote those ideas and suggestions. It strives to act as an agency that has a from-the-bottom-up grassroots view of its activities.

"We get many visits from people from across the country, and they're very taken by our shelter and our staff and the programs we provide," said Bond. "The city (of Guelph) is not aware of the reputation the Guelph Humane Society has coast-to-coast."

Volunteers and active members may be the heart and soul of GHS, but it is the staff who come face-to-face with the public the Society serves. And much of the success the Society has achieved is due to their ability to act in a professional manner, promoting the highest ideals of the humane movement.

Providing humane and animal control services in Guelph isn't just a matter of running after cats and dogs. It is often much more, as the following anecdotes from animal control officer Michelle Jackson illustrate:

Shooting the bull?

There was a time when Michelle Jackson had to shoot the bull, . . . er, that is she had to shoot the bull with a bull, if you get the drift.

There it was, the biggest darn bull ever to graze in the backyard of a Guelph home. The bull looked determined yet apprehensive, and the homeowner equally determined and apprehensive.

It was clearly a test of wits because in the final analysis, if the bull wanted to rage, it would be the homeowner and the garden he chose to protect that would suffer great physical injury.

"The bull had squeezed through a barb wire fence adjoining the unfortunate man's property and that of a beef farmer," said Jackson. "I advised the man to hold back and not do anything rash while I went and got the farmer.

"When I returned with the farmer, she grabbed a rope and with a bucket of grain in hand, we coaxed the bull back into the field to rejoin the herd.

"It was a touchy situation, but it's also likely the only time I've had – or ever will have – a 'cow at large' call."

A Tail of Squirrels

Then there's the tail of the 'Siamese squirrels' which amazed Jackson, and everyone who came in contact with five baby squirrels found in a backyard with their tails joined.

"I asked the caller to repeat this one for me," said Jackson, "but that's indeed what I found when I arrived.

"Five baby squirrels were stuck together at the tail by a tangle of nesting material. The poor mother was quite distraught about the situation and could do little.

"The babies all wanted to go in five separate directions, which only added to the confusion. As soon as we untangled one, it would become wrapped around a bush or a tree.

"Finally, I had all five in a gloved hand, placed them in a cage and took them to OVC. The people at the college were just as surprised as I was, and could hardly believe what I was saying, until I arrived and showed them the problem.

"The babies were tranquilized while several students worked on them. Forty-five minutes later I had five separate but groggy squirrels. I waited a half hour for them to wake up before I returned them to mother, who, as might be expected, was in ecstasy and quite relieved to see them again.

"That's what you call a happy ending."

The stories told by Michelle Jackson are only two of many hundreds GHS staff members become a part of every day at the shelter, or on the streets of Guelph.

"For the past 100 years, the Society has been working to achieve as many of those happy endings as possible," said John Runge. But much work remains, including issues involving performing animals, pet overpopulation, the role of pet stores in society, cat control, the on-going struggle to battle rabies, and the need for a comprehensive strategy to deal with wildlife and the loss of its habitat to urban expansion.

As GHS celebrates its centennial in 1993, it looks forward to a future with a dedicated membership. The strong sense of community that brought the Society to this celebration will ensure that it continues in the struggle against cruelty, working for the welfare of all animal species.

Officers of the Guelph Humane Society 1893-1993

Name	Position	Year(s)
Lt.-Col. Nathaniel Higinbotham	**President**	**1893-1896**
James Goldie	1st Vice-president	1893-95
Miss Annie Keating	2nd Vice-president	1893
William Tytler	Treasurer Secretary Pro Tem (Organizing meeting)	1893
Dr. Brock	2nd Vice-president	1896-97
E. R. Bollert	**President**	**1897-1900**
Mrs. Thomas Goldie	1st Vice-president	1897-1926[1]
Frank W. Galbraith	**President** 2nd Vice-president Secretary	**1900 - 02** 1897 1893 - 96
Joseph Sharpe	Secretary/Treasurer	1897 - 98
A. S. Allan	**President**	**1902 -19**
Janet C. Melvin	Secretary	1902- 04
William Laidlaw	Treasurer	1918- 26
John Armstrong	**President**	**1919 - 21**
Rev. (Capt.) C. H. Buckland	1st Vice-president	1920
Rev. (Capt.) G. W. A. Little	Second Vice-president	1920
Dr. N. C. Wallace	**President**	**1921-26**
Ex-Mayor Stephens	President - Humane Educational League	1925
J. S. Millar	President - Humane Educational League	1926
Dr. W.R.J. Fowler	**President**	**1927 - 29**
Maude Pentelow	Vice-president	1927-31
William Laidlaw	Corresponding Secretary	1927 - 42
Mary Graesser	Secretary - Humane Educational League	1925 - 26
	Recording Secretary - Humane Society	1927 - 43

[1] Mrs. Goldie's tenure as first vice-president and member of the executive committee is vouched for by Dr. Norman Wallace, president of the society from 1921-26. Wallace notes in the 1926 annual report, the last before the society was split: "In 1897, she was elected First Vice-president, and has held this office continuously for thirty years." However, the 1920 annual meeting minutes show Rev. (Capt.) Buckland was elected to the office.

A Century of Caring

Officers of the Guelph Humane Society 1893-1993

Name	Position	Year(s)
Frank H. Cooke	Treasurer	1929-42
Canon W. G. Davis	**President**	**1930 - 31**
Dr. Lionel Stevenson[2]	**President**	**1932 - 41**
Rev. F. H. Wase	Vice-president	1932-33
W. G. Howell	Vice-president	1935-37
Dr. H. D. Wilson	Vice-president	1934
Harold Storey Nicklin	Vice-president	1938-49[3]
Frank K. Baker	**President**	**1942**
Frank H. Cooke	**President**	**1943 - 73**
Mrs. James (Marion) McFaulds	Vice-president	1951-54
F. H. Young	Vice-president	1954-69
E.C. Pettifer	2nd Vice-president	1955
Dr. Alan J. Cawley	Vice-president	1969
A. McMaster Laird	Vice-president	1970
Mrs. E. C. (Elizabeth) Pettifer	Treasurer	1952 - 72
Mrs. L. P. (Eva) Davies	Secretary	1943 - 67
Marion Hawkins / Mrs. E.C. Pettifer	Secretary	1968
J. C. Andrews	Secretary	1969-74
Sandra Jefferies Bond	**President**	**1973 - 77**
Dr. Ron Downey	Vice-president	1973 - 77
Susan (Burns) Andrews	Treasurer	1973 - 76
Ellen (Carney) Anderson	Secretary	1974 - 75
Susan Toldness	Secretary	1975 - 78
R. L. (Bob) Rutter	**President**	**1978**
Joanna Watkin	Vice-president	1978

[2] A faculty member at the Ontario Veterinary College, Stevenson also served as the provincial zoologist.
[3] The annual meeting report of 1948 does not list a vice-president.

Officers of the Guelph Humane Society 1893-1993

Name	Position	Year(s)
Janet Daly	Treasurer	1976 - 92
Joanna Watkin	**President**	**1979 - 81**
Dr. Ron Downey	Vice-president	1979 - 80
Margaret Hauser	Vice-president	1981 - 86
Bill DeShane	Secretary	1978 - 80
Grace Gray	Secretary	1981
Dr. Ron Downey	**President**	**1982**
Edna Jones	Secretary	1982 - 83
Joanna Watkin	**President**	**1983 - 84**
Sandra Jefferies Bond	**President**	**1985 - 90**
Gail Howson	Secretary	1984 - 86
Margaret Hauser	Secretary	1987 - 89
John Runge	Vice-president	1987 - 88
Margaret Hauser	Secretary	1987 - 92
Eleanor Burchill	Vice-president	1989 - 90
John Runge	**President**	**1991 - 92**
Cheryl Starr	Vice-president	1991 - 92

Inspectors/Shelter Managers

Name	Position	Year(s)
Thomas Elliott	Inspector	1894-96
Rev. James Lediard	Agent[4]	1897
Major Merewether	Inspector	1900-05[5]
Rev. P.C. Laverton Harris	Inspector	1906-09
Rev. Amos Tovell	Inspector	1909-26

[4] Reference contained in the 1897 annual report of Neglected and Dependent Children of Ontario.
[5] Minutes of the 1905 annual meeting states the society was having difficulty in hiring someone to fill a vacancy for an inspector.

A Century of Caring

Officers of the Guelph Humane Society 1893-1993

Name	Position	Year(s)
Geoffrey Fraser	Inspector	1927-47
G.L. (Len) Shaw	Inspector	1947-65
Philip Griffiths[6]	Inspector	
James Cosgrove	Inspector	
Edward Latta	Inspector	
Sean Pennylegion	Shelter Manager	1973-77
Suzanne Money	Shelter Manager	1977-78
Gillian DeLaFranier	Shelter Manager	1978-79
Lorna Ronald	Shelter Manager	1980-82 / 1986-93
Kathy Elliot	Shelter Manager	1982-83
Karen Kowalchuk	Shelter Manager	1984-86

[6] There are gaps in employment records for the period between 1965-73. Those who can be identified from various documented sources are listed in no particular order.